Study Guide

for

American Government and Politics Today

1999-2000 Edition

**Steffen W. Schmidt, Mack C. Shelley II, and
Barbara A. Bardes**

Prepared by

James Perkins
San Antonio College

West/Wadsworth
I(T)P® An International Thomson Publishing Company

Belmont, CA • Albany, NY • Boston • Cincinnati • Johannesburg • London • Madrid • Melbourne
Mexico City • New York • Pacific Grove, CA • Scottsdale, AZ • Singapore • Tokyo • Toronto

Printed in the United States of America.
1 2 3 4 5 6 7 8 9 10

For more information, contact Wadsworth Publishing Company, 10 Davis Drive, Belmont, CA 94002, or electronically at http://www.wadsworth.com

International Thomson Publishing Europe
Berkshire House
168-173 High Holborn
London, WC1V 7AA, United Kingdom

International Thomson Editores
Seneca, 53
Colonia Polanco
11560 México D.F. México

Nelson ITP, Australia
102 Dodds Street
South Melbourne
Victoria 3205 Australia

International Thomson Publishing Asia
60 Albert Street #15-01
Albert Complex
Singapore 189969

Nelson Canada
1120 Birchmount Road
Scarborough, Ontario
Canada M1K 5G4

International Thomson Publishing Southern Africa
Building 18, Constantia Square
138 Sixteenth Road, P.O. Box 2459
Halfway House, 1685 South Africa

International Thomson Publishing Japan
Hirakawa-cho Kyowa Building, 3F
2-2-1 Hirakawa-cho
Chiyoda-ku
Tokyo 102, Japan

ISBN 0-534-55318-4

Contents

Preface

This *Study Guide* is part of a comprehensive instructional package designed to accompany the eighth edition of *American Government and Politics Today, 1999-2000 edition*. The preface to the *text* gives an overview of the Special Pedagogical Aids and High-Interest Features designed to promote mastery of key concepts in American government. I suggest that you read over this section of the text very carefully before beginning to read and study Chapter 1.

This *Guide* coordinates with a supplemental CD-ROM *America at Odds* that your instructor may assign. Even if the CD-ROM is not assigned, I encourage you to check with your bookstore (you will need the ISBN 0-534-53626-3) and purchase it independently. Through videos, capsule histories, interviews, and interactive quizzes, the CD-ROM will expand your understanding of the theoretical concepts and make them come alive as contemporary issues.

A new part of the comprehensive instructional package is the *Electronic Study Guide* which has exam questions on the **Internet**. Designed in an interactive format, the electonic study guide facilitates answering questions in a more realistic examination setting and receiving rapid feed-back on your mastery of the concepts.

This print version of the *Study Guide* begins with a "Chapter Summary" outlining the important concepts of each chapter in the text. "Key Terms," page-referenced to the text's margin definitions, follow the outline. Extra space after each term allows you to define the term and begin to assemble an understanding of the important concepts.

A "Practice Exam" designed to test your understanding of important concepts concludes each chapter in the *Guide*. This exam contains both objective and subjective questions. The objective questions—fill-in-the-blank, true/false, and multiple-choice—are page-referenced to the text to allow verifying your answers. Short essay questions focus your attention on synthesizing key concepts. Answers to all the questions appear at the end of each chapter.

I hope that you find this *Guide* useful in learning the complexities of American government and politics. And I wish you success. More than ever, our country needs informed citizens who will take an active role in the democratic process.

Chapter 1
American Government and Politics: Stability and Change

CHAPTER SUMMARY

Political Change in the United States

The election system in the United States allows us to change the balance of power in the national government, every two years, if we choose. In 1994 and 1996, the nation chose to continue a policy of divided government with a Republican-controlled Congress and a Democratic President [p. 5].

What is Politics?

Politics is defined by Harold Lasswell as, "Who gets what, when, and how?" in a society. David Easton defines it as the "authoritative allocation of values" for a society. The authors of the text define politics as the reference to conflict and conflict resolution in society. Conflict is always present in society for three major reasons [page 7]:

- differences in beliefs or ideologies
- differences in the perceived goals of the society
- scarce resources that prevent society from satisfying every want and need.

The Need for Government and Power

Government refers to the institutions that resolve conflicts and allocate values. These institutions require authority, legitimacy, and power in order to accomplish their purpose of resolving conflict.

- Authority is the feature of a leader or institution that compels obedience. Usually this obedience derives from legitimacy.
- Legitimacy is the status conferred by the people on the officials, acts, and institutions of the government if the people believe that the actions taken are legal and right.
- Power is the ability to cause others to modify their behavior and conform to what the power holder wants. To sum up, authority is the legitimate use of power.

Who Governs?

A fundamental question of politics asks who makes political decisions for a society? Anarchy exists when no government exists and individuals must try to resolve conflicts on their own. In an oligarchy, decisions are made by a few members of the elite. An elite is defined as an upper socioeconomic class. Aristocracy refers to decisions made by the best suited in terms of wealth, education, intelligence, and family prestige. In a democracy, decisions are made by the majority of people [p. 9]. Direct democracy exists when people make decisions in person, as in the New England town meeting. A possible danger of direct democracy is mob rule, in which the majority abuse the rights of minority groups [p. 10]. This danger led our society to create a republic or representative democracy, in which representatives are elected by the people to make and enforce laws.

The three principles essential for democratic government in our society are [p. 11]:

- universal suffrage—the right of all adults to vote for their representatives;
- majority rule and the protection of minority rights;
- limited government—governments authority limited by a written document or widely held beliefs.

Do We Have a Democracy?

Elite theory has suggested that society is ruled by a small number of wealthy people who exercise power in their self-interest. Because elites resist any change in their status, the primary goal of such a society is stability [p. 13]. Pluralism theory has proposed that conflict in society occurs among interest groups. Political decision-making is determined by bargaining and compromise among groups. Hyperpluralism has suggested that interest groups can become so powerful that their competitive struggles with each other virtually paralyze society [p. 14].

Ideas and Politics: Political Culture

Political Culture can be defined as a patterned set of ideas, values, and ways of thinking about government and politics. The process by which such beliefs and values are transmitted to immigrants and our children is called Political Socialization [p. 15]. The Fundamental Values of the American political culture can be defined as [p. 16-17]:

- liberty—the greatest freedom of individuals that is consistent with the freedom of other individuals in society;
- equality—all people are of equal worth; and
- property—the right of individual ownership.

Political culture holds society together by persuading people to support the existing political process [p. 17-18]. See Figure 1-1 on p. 20.

The Changing Face of America

The context of the American society is changing as Americans age, become more diverse, and need new laws and policies. In 1999,

- almost 13% of the population was sixty-five years or older. Combined with low birth rates, this trend holds important implications for retirement and pension systems, including Social Security [p. 20-21];
- over 75% of the population lived in urban areas; and25% of children lived in one-parent households.
- Hispanics, African Americans, and Asian Americans have become a larger portion of the United States population because of higher birth rates and immigration [p. 21]. See Figure 1-3 on p. 21.
- The number of persons in prisons has grown to over 1,200,000. Militia groups opposed to the government have increased in number, membership, and violent action against the government.
- National surveys have found that about 20% of all Americans are barely literate [p. 23].

Ideas and Politics: Ideology

Ideology can be defined as a comprehensive and logical set of beliefs about the nature of people and institutions, and the role of government. American ideology has been dominated by two moderate ideologies: liberalism and conservatism [p. 23]. Liberalism is the belief that, in part, supports government action to improve the welfare of individuals, supports civil rights, and accepts political and social change. Conservatism is the belief that, in part, supports a limited role for government assistance to individuals, supports traditional values, and expresses a cautious response to change.

America's Politics: Issues For the New Century

As diversity increases, our nation struggles to maintain a cohesive society and increase the level of participation in the political process. The new century will require the creation of institutions and policies to deal with global markets and global electronic communication on the Internet [p. 26].

KEY TERMS

authority—p. 8

conservatism—p. 23

democracy—p. 9

direct democracy—p. 9

elite theory—p. 12

equality—p. 15

government—p. 7

ideology—p. 23

C D-RO M *AMERICA AT ODDS*

IMMIGRATION. The first interactive module deals with the topic of immigration, and is thus especially relevant to themes of diversity and hyperpluralism contained in the first chapter. The module contains interactive questions and audio clips about issues such as California's Proposition 187, recently declared unconstitutional by a federal district court, and the Illegal Immigration Act of 1996, which has inspired controversy around the issues of patrolling the nation's borders and the rights of illegal immigrants. A ten-question interactive multiple-choice quiz reinforces key points in the material.

PRACTICE EXAM

[Answers appear at the end of this chapter.]

Fill-In-The-Blank. Supply the missing word[s] or term[s] to complete the sentence.

1. Definitions of politics try to explain how human beings regulate _____ within their society.

2. The feature of a leader or an institution that compels obedience is called _____.

3. The ancient Greek city-state of Athens is considered the historical model for _____ _____.

4. The U. S. Constitution created a form of republican government known as a _____.

5. From the elite perspective, the goal of government is _____.

6. In the pluralist view, politics is the struggle among _____ _____.

7. A fundamental source of political socialization is the _____.

8. Democracy, liberty, equality, and property form the core of American _____.

9. Immigration, as a percentage of total U.S. population growth, since 1970, has _____.

5

10. Within the American electorate, the two most commonly held ideologies are _____ and

_____.

True/False. Circle the appropriate letter to indicate if the statement is true or false.

1. T   F   Political scientists are able to agree that politics involves the resolution of social conflict.
2. T   F   In democratic nations, most citizens comply with the law because they accept the authority of the government and its officials.
3. T   F   Direct democracy in ancient Athens was considered the ideal form of democracy.
4. T   F   James Madison strongly advocated a pure democracy for the American political system.
5. T   F   In a representative democracy, the people hold the ultimate power over the government through the election process.
6. T   F   The elite perspective sees the mass population as actively involved in the decisions of government.
7. T   F   A democratic system paralyzed by the struggle among interest groups is called hyperpluralism.
8. T   F   The basic guarantee of liberties to citizens of the American political system is found in the body of the U.S. Constitution.
9. T   F   The 1990 census indicates a very low rate of U.S. population growth.
10. T   F   Immigrants are likely to shape American politics in the future.

Multiple-choice. Circle the correct response.

1. All definitions of politics try to explain how human beings regulate
    a. natural resources within their society.
    b. good and evil within a complex society.
    c. self-expression.
    d. conflict within their society.

2. The form of government that controls all political, social, and economic life is called a[n]
    a. democratic regime.
    b. socialist regime.
    c. totalitarian regime.
    d. oligarchy.

3. When all individuals make their own rules for behavior, and there are no laws and no government,

   a. pure democracy prevails.

   b. anarchy exists.

   c. an oligarchy exists.

   d. the ideal form of government prevails.

4. The Athenian model of government was considered

   a. the ideal form of democracy.

   b. a weak and ineffective form of government.

   c. the reason why Roman legions were able to conquer Greece.

   d. the forerunner of communism.

5. An initiative is a procedure by which voters can

   a. directly make laws.

   b. remove elected officials.

   c. propose a law or constitutional amendment.

   d. place candidates on a ballot.

6. The U. S. Constitution creates a form of republican government known as a

   a. pure democracy.

   b. confederation.

   c. representative democracy.

   d. majoritarian system.

7. A central feature of the American governmental system is

   a. the supremacy of Congress over the other branches.

   b. control of the airwaves.

   c. the tendency to provide foreign aid to every country.

   d. equality of every individual before the law.

8. To ensure that majority rule does not become oppressive, modern democracies

   a. provide guarantees of minority rights.

   b. have constitutions that are difficult to amend.

   c. use plurality voting for most decisions.

   d. hold free, competitive elections.

9. The U.S. Constitution

   a. does not set forth enough detail about how the government should function.

   b. is too open to interpretation, which creates confusion for government leaders.

   c. has more amendments than any other national constitution.

   d. sets forth the fundamental structure of the government and the limits to its power.

10. According to the elite perspective, the primary goal of government should be stability, because
    a. elites do not want any change in their status.
    b. stability is the only thing that can ensure a good life.
    c. instability will create greater welfare problems.
    d. unstable government is more vulnerable to foreign invasion.

11. Pluralist theory rests on the idea that decisions are made in American politics by
    a. the mass population.
    b. the governing elites.
    c. the wealthy.
    d. the competition between groups trying to gain benefits for their members.

12. When the needs of a group control government decision-making to the detriment of the general population, we have a condition known as
    a. legislative fiat.
    b. democratization of groups.
    c. hyperpluralism.
    d. factionalism.

13. The pattern of political beliefs and values characteristic of a community or population is referred to as
    a. public opinion.
    b. democratic heritage.
    c. political culture.
    d. consensus of opinion.

14. The process by which Americans accept a single set of values for their political system is called
    a. enculturation.
    b. education.
    c. political socialization.
    d. propaganda.

15. Democracy, liberty, equality, and property are
    a. concepts that no longer have meaning in modern political systems.
    b. now thought to be unattainable in a modern pluralistic society.
    c. concepts that lie at the core of American political culture.
    d. concepts that encompass all of our political heritage.

Short Essay Questions. Briefly address the major concepts raised by the following questions.

1. Explain the role of politics in an organized society.
2. Explain the origins of democracy and the different types of democracy.

3. Define the fundamental elements of the American political culture.

4. Compare and contrast the concepts of liberalism and conservatism.

ANSWERS TO THE PRACTICE EXAM

Fill-in-the-Blank.

1. conflict [p. 7]
2. authority [p. 8]
3. direct democracy [p. 10]
4. representative democracy [p. 11]
5. stability [p. 13]

6. interest groups [p. 14]
7. family [p. 15]
8. political culture [p. 16]
9. increased [p. 22]
10. liberalism, conservatism [p. 23]

True/False.

1. T [p. 6]
2. T [p. 8]
3. T [p. 9]
4. F [p. 9]
5. T [p. 10]
6. F [p. 10]
7. T [p. 14]
8. F [p. 11]
9. T [p. 17]
10. T [p. 20]

Multiple-Choice.

1. d [p. 6]
2. c [p. 8]
3. b [p. 9]
4. a [p. 9]
5. c [p. 10]
6. c [p. 10]
7. d [p. 11]
8. a [p. 11]
9. d [p. 12]
10. a [p. 13]
11. d [p. 13]
12. c [p. 14]
13. c [p. 14]
14. c [p. 14]
15. c [p. 17]

Short Essay Answers.

An adequate short answer consists of several paragraphs that discuss the concepts addressed by the question. Always demonstrate your knowledge of the ideas by giving examples. The following represent the major ideas that should be included in these short essays.

1. Explain the role of politics in an organized society [p. 6-8].
   - Definitions of politics: Harold Lasswell, David Easton, and your authors
   - Government and power
   - Authority and legitimacy
2. Explain the origins of democracy and the different types of democracy [p. 10-12].
   - Athenian model of direct democracy
   - Representative democracy
   - Principles of Western representative democracy
   - Constitutional democracy

3. Define the fundamental values of the American political culture [p. 15-17].

    *   Liberty
    *   Equality
    *   Property

4. Compare and contrast the concepts of liberalism and conservatism [p. 23-26].

    *   Ideology—a set of ideas about the goal of politics
    *   Liberals
        ◊   Positive government action to solve social problems
        ◊   Advocates for civil rights
        ◊   Advocates for social change
    *   Conservatives
        ◊   Faith in the private sector to solve most social problems
        ◊   Advocates for individual action to protect rights
        ◊   Advocates for a return to traditional values

Chapter 2
The Constitution

CHAPTER SUMMARY

Initial Colonizing efforts

The first British settlement in North American was Roanoke Island which mysteriously disappeared. Recent research has indicated that a severe drought must have wiped out the colony. Jamestown, Virginia and Plymouth, Massachusetts, in 1607 and 1620, respectively, were the first successful settlements. Additional settlements followed in Massachusetts and Connecticut. See the Milestones in Early U.S. Political History on p. 35.

British Restrictions and Colonial Grievances

To pay for the French and Indian War expenses, the British government decided to tax the colonists. The Sugar Act in 1764 and Stamp Act in 1765 led to the Boston Tea Party, which caused the British Parliament to pass the Coercive or (Intolerable) Acts in 1774 [p. 36].

The Colonial Response: The Continental Congresses

The colonists responded to the British by holding the First Continental Congress, which issued a petition of grievances, and attempted to create committees to bring the colonists together. Fighting had already occurred between the colonists and the British when, in 1775, the Second Continental Congress met and established an army under Commander-in-Chief George Washington [p. 36].

Declaring Independence

In early 1776, the Second Continental Congress approved the Resolution of Independence in order to establish legitimacy and seek foreign military aid. The Second Congress assigned Thomas Jefferson the task of writing a formal declaration of independence. This *Declaration of Independence* was approved on July 4, 1776, and contained three major principles based on the ideas of English political philosopher John Locke. These concepts were natural rights, consent of the governed, and the right to change the government.

The Rise of Republicanism

Colonists, who called themselves Republicans, were opposed to any strong central government. From 1776 to 1780, Republicans were a powerful political force in the creation of strong state governments.

The Articles of Confederation: Our First Form of Government

In 1781, the Articles of Confederation established a voluntary association of independent states to address national concerns. See Figure 2-1, p. 39, and Table 2-1, p. 40, for information about the powers of this form of government. The lack of taxing authority made government under the Articles too weak to survive and Shay's Rebellion in 1786 spurred political leaders to take action [p. 41].

Drafting the Constitution

The Annapolis Convention was called in 1786 to discuss the weaknesses of the national government.

At this meeting, a call went out to all the states to attend a general convention in Philadelphia in May, 1787 [p. 42]. Delegates from every state except Rhode Island attended the Philadelphia convention. The delegates were mostly nationalists, but included monarchists, democratic nationalists, non-democratic nationalists, and advocates of strong state governmenst. The debates, which began the first day, produced two major plans:

- the Virginia Plan, which proposed an entirely new national government favoring big states, and
- the New Jersey Plan, which was an amendment to the Articles of Confederation.

The deadlock between these two proposals was broken by the "Great Compromise," brokered by the Connecticut delegation, which called for a bicameral legislature for a new form of national government.

Slavery and other issues between the agrarian South and the mercantile North were resolved by other compromises, including the Three-Fifths Compromise [p. 44]. The final agreement included:

- separation of powers, sometimes known as the Madisonian model,
- a system of checks and balances [See Figure 2-2, p. 47.]
- an electoral college to elect the president [p. 46].

The Final Document

The Constitution was approved on September 17, 1787, by thirty-nine delegates. The document established five fundamental principles:

- popular sovereignty
- a republican form of government
- limited government
- separation of powers
- a federal system.

The Difficult Road to Ratification

In the battle for ratification, the Federalists, who favored ratification, opposed the Anti-Federalists, who rejected the Constitution as it was drafted. Hamilton, Madison, and Jay, wrote the Federalists Papers, which influenced the success of the ratification effort [p. 48]. In 1788, the ninth state, New Hampshire, ratified the Constitution and sealed the formal acceptance of our national government. See Table 2-2 on p. 49 for the ratification vote in each of the states.

The Bill of Rights

Ratification of the Constitution was probably dependent on the Federalists' promise to protect individual liberties by amending the Constitution. James Madison culled through recommendations from state conventions to produce what became the Bill of Rights. The 10 amendments of the Bill of Rights were ratified in 1791 [p. 50-51]. An interesting note, one of the amendments originally proposed was not ratified until 1992 when it became the 27th amendment to the Constitution.

The Motives of the Framers

In historian Charles Beard's book, *An Economic Interpretation of the Constitution of the United States*, Beard points out that because the delegates to the Constitutional Convention were predominately wealthy members of the upper class, they may have supported a strong government in order to protect their property. The question remains whether a popular majority supported the Constitution [p. 51-54].

Altering the Constitution: The Formal Amendment Process

Amending the Constitution is a two-step process. The first step is proposing a new amendment, either 1) by a two-thirds vote in both houses of Congress, or 2) by a national convention called by Congress at the request of two-thirds of the states. The second step is ratifying the amendment. Ratification is accomplished by either a three-fourths vote of the state legislatures or by a three-fourths vote of state conventions called to ratify the amendment. See Figure 2-3 on p. 54.

Congress has considered more than 11,000 amendments, of which 33 have been submitted for ratification and only 27 have been ratified. [See Table 2-3 on p. 55.] Since 1919, most proposed amendments have carried a seven-year ratification limit, but the 27th amendment, ratified in 1992, took 203 years [p. 56].

Informal Methods of Constitutional Change

While there been have few formal amendments to the constitution over the centuries, informal change has occurred on a more frequent basis. These informal changes have been by legislation passed by Congress under the commerce clause, and Article III, Section 1 of the constitution. The constitution has changed by the creation of executive agreements by Presidents to conduct foreign policy. The Supreme Court has claimed the power of judicial review in the case of Marbury v. Madison (1803). P. 58. Finally, through the usage in day to day government activities, interpretation, custom and tradition have influenced the meaning of the constitution.

The Constitution: Issues for the New Century

The age of global technology, information, and communication will severely test the flexibility of the constitution to respond to the challenges of the 21sr century. It also appears that the balance of power between the states and national government will be a key issue in the new century.

KEY TERMS

anti-federalist—p. 48

bicameral legislature—p. 44

separation of powers—p. 46

state—p. 38

supremacy doctrine—p. 45

unicameral legislature—p. 38

CD-ROM *AMERICA AT ODDS*

THE CONSTITUTION AND CYBERSPACE.   The second interactive module presents the historical concept of free speech, and the impact that the Internet has had on free speech issues. It discusses the 1996 Communication Decency Act, which was ruled unconstitutional by the Supreme Court. It also discusses strategies for families to protect children from pornography on the Internet. A ten-question interactive multiple-choice quiz reinforces key points in the material.

PRACTICE EXAM

(Answers appear at the end of this chapter.)

Fill-in-the-Blank. Supply the missing word(s) or term(s) to complete the sentence.

1.   The passage of the Coercive Acts by the British Parliament was a response to the _____.

2.   The rights of "life, liberty, and the pursuit of happiness" are referred to as _____.

3.   A voluntary association of independent states is referred to as _____.

4.   The plan of government that introduced the idea of a bicameral legislature was the _____.

5. The agreement that resolved the differences between the large and small states over representation in the

   new government was the _____.

6. Nowhere in the _____ are the words slavery or slaves used.

7. _____ was the name given to those who favored the adoption of the new constitution.

8. The _____ _____ are considered by many to be the best example of

   political theorizing ever produced in the United States.

9. The _____ was one of the two "lost" amendments of the twelve bill of rights

   amendments that originally went to the states in 1789.

10. The _____ _____ is the only court specifically created in the Constitution.

True/False. Circle the appropriate letter to indicate if the statement is true or false.
1. T F The Mayflower Compact embodied the idea of majority rule as a theory of government.
2. T F Thomas Paine's *Common Sense* popularized the idea of independence from Great Britain.
3. T F According to the Declaration of Independence, these United Colonies are, and of right ought
          to be, free and independent states.
4. T F The most fundamental weakness of the Articles of Confederation was the inability of the
          to raise money for the militia.
5. T F A majority of delegates to the Constitutional convention favored a strong central government.
6. T F The Virginia plan called for each state to have equal representation in the new government.
7. T F The Anti-Federalists believed that the central government should be strengthened over the
          states, because the states were apt to abuse personal liberties.

8. T   F   The delegates to the Constitutional Convention represented a good cross-section of eighteenth-century American society.

9. T   F   Only a 4/5 vote of all of the state legislatures can formally amend the Constitution.

10. T   F   An informal way to amend the Constitution is by judicial review.

Multiple-Choice. Circle the correct response.

1. The "lost colony" was

    a. Roanoke.

    b. Richmond.

    c. Jamestown.

    d. Portsmouth.

2. The last of the thirteen colonies to be established was

    a. Rhode Island.

    b. Connecticut.

    c. New Hampshire.

    d. Georgia.

3. The British government imposed taxes on the American colonies to pay for

    a. war with Spain.

    b. the costs of westward expansion of colonies.

    c. the costs of the French and Indian War.

    d. the costs of exploring India.

4. Thomas Paine's pamphlet, *Common Sense*,

    a. called for a cessation of hostilities against the British.

    b. pointed out in "common sense" terms why America should break with Britain.

    c. was a British propaganda tool to gain popular consent to their governing of the colonies.

    d. apparently had very little effect on popular opinion about the revolution.

5. One of John Locke's revolutionary ideas was that people have

    a. a right to a secure job.

    b. a right to welfare if they need it.

    c. natural rights.

    d. a right to checks and balances in government.

6. During the Revolutionary War, the _____ influenced the creation of state governments

    a. Federalists.

    b. Democrats.

    c. Republicans.

    d. Monarchists.

7. The government under the Articles of Confederation Congress included a

    a. president, but no congress.

    b. congress and a president.

    c. unicameral legislature.

    d. strong central government.

8. Under the Articles of Confederation,

    a. each state had one vote.

    b. the national courts were the supreme authority.

    c. the congress imposed heavy taxes.

    d. the president ultimately controlled the government.

9. An important accomplishment of the Articles of Confederation was

    a. the creation of a common currency.

    b. settling states' claims to western lands.

    c. the creation of national tax collections.

    d. the creation of a strong national army.

10. Under the Article of Confederation, the Congress had the power to

    a. declare war and make peace.

    b. draft soldiers into military service.

    c. compel states to pay their share of national government costs.

    d. regulate interstate and foreign commerce.

11. Shay's rebellion demonstrated that the central government

    a. had the capability to protect citizens from riots and civil unrest.

    b. could not protect the citizenry from armed rebellion.

    c. dared not confront state militias.

    d. could easily incite citizens to riot.

12. The only state that refused to send delegates to the Constitutional Convention was

    a. New Hampshire.

    b. Rhode Island.

    c. New York.

    d. Virginia.

13. The proceedings in the Constitutional Convention were kept secret because

    a. the delegates were doing something illegal.

    b. the public would not understand the issues involved and would create confusion.

    c. all meetings of this nature must be secret.

    d. if they were public, the delegates might have a more difficult time compromising on issues.

14. The Great Compromise

    a. resulted in the Bill of Rights being added to the Constitution.

    b. broke the deadlock between the large and small states over representation in the new congress.

    c. established the Electoral College as the vehicle for electing the president.

    d. allowed George Washington to be nominated and elected the first president.

15. The Madisonian model of a government scheme refers to

    a. direct democracy.

    b. judicial review.

    c. a separation of powers.

    d. the supremacy of national laws over state laws.

Short Essay Questions. Briefly address the major concepts raised by the following questions.

1. Identify the milestone political documents that moved the colonies from the Mayflower Compact to the Constitutional Convention.

2. Trace the events and circumstances that led to the Revolutionary War.

3. Summarize the events leading to the call for a Constitutional Convention.

4. Explain the compromises over the organization of the government designed by the delegates to the Constitutional Convention.

ANSWERS TO THE PRACTICE EXAM

Fill-in-the-Blank.

1. Boston Tea Party [p. 36]

2. Natural rights [p. 37]

3. Confederation [p. 38]

4. Virginia Plan [p. 44]

5. Great Compromise [p. 45]

6. Constitution [p. 46]

7. Federalists [p. 48]

8. Federalists Papers [p. 49]

9. 27th Amendment [p. 57]

10. Supreme Court [p. 59]

True/False.

1. T [p. 35]	3. T [p. 37]	5. T [p. 42]	7. F [p. 49]	9. F [p. 55]
2. T [p. 36]	4. T [p. 40]	6. F [p. 44]	8. F [p. 54]	10. T [p. 59]

Multiple Choice.

1. a [p. 33]	4. b [p. 36]	7. c [p. 39]	10. a [p. 40]	13. d [p. 42]
2. d [p. 35]	5. c [p. 37]	8. a [p. 39]	11. b [p. 41]	14. b [p. 45]
3. c [p. 35]	6. a [p. 38]	9. b [p. 39]	12. b [p. 41]	15. c [p. 46]

Chapter 2   The Constitution

Short Essay Answers.

An adequate short answer consists of several paragraphs that discuss the concepts addressed by the question. Always demonstrate your knowledge of the ideas by giving examples. The following represent the major ideas that should be included in these short essays.

1. Identify the milestone political documents that moved the colonies from the Mayflower Compact to the Constitutional Convention.
    *   Refer to the time line on page 35 to give you a good overview of the question.
    *   The Mayflower Compact of 1620 was a political agreement derived from the consent of the people.
    *   The Fundamental Orders of Connecticut, 1639, was the first written constitution.
    *   The Massachusetts Body of Liberties, 1641, was the first constitution to include protection of individual rights.
    *   The Pennsylvania Charter of Privileges, 1701, contained a constitution and bill of rights and offered a precedent and rationale for our national Constitution.
    *   The Declaration of Independence, 1776, advocated independence from Great Britain.
    *   The Articles of Confederation, 1781, described the first attempt at an independent national government based on a confederation.

2. Trace the events and circumstances that led to the Revolutionary War.
    *   Address this question in chronological/historical order.
    *   Explain the reasons for British restrictions represented by the Sugar Act, Stamp Act, and Coercive Act.
    *   Describe the colonial responses of the First and Second Continental Congresses; Paine's *Common Sense*.
    *   Describe the Resolution of Independence and Declaration of Independence.

3. Summarize the events that led to the call for the Constitutional Convention.
    *   Explain the development of the Articles of Confederation structure and the distribution of power.
    *   Explain the weaknesses of the Articles of Confederation as seen in the lack of good will among the states and the inability to tax for national needs.
    *   Explain the impact of Shay's Rebellion

4. Explain the compromises that evolved at the Constitutional Convention and affected the organization of the government.
    *   Discuss the various proposed structures for the new government as seen in the Virginia Plan and the New Jersey Plan
    *   Describe the Great Compromise.
    *   Discuss the distribution of governmental power represented by Madison's theories of a separation of powers and a system of checks and balances.

Chapter 3
Federalism

CHAPTER SUMMARY

Government in the United States consists of one national government, fifty state governments, and thousands of local governments [see Table 3-1 on p. 85].

Three systems of Government

There are three basic ways of organizing governmental structures and the flow of power. See Figure 3-1 on p. 87. A unitary system places ultimate governmental authority in the national government. A confederate system links power in a league of independent states. A federal system divides authority between a national government and state government [p. 85-86].

Why Federalism?

The United States developed a federal system because it was a practical solution. Federalism retained state traditions and local power while creating a strong national government, and solved the problems produced by geographical size and regional isolation. Other arguments for federalism point out that it diffused political dissatisfaction among the different governments; provided a training ground for future national leaders; allowed diverse regional groups to develop; and brought government closer to the people [p. 87]

Not every political viewpoint supported federalism. Arguments against federalism point out that on the one hand, it allowed national powers to expand at the expense of states, while one the other, provided a way for powerful state and local interests to block national progress and deny equal rights for minorities [p. 88].

The Constitutional Basis for American Federalism

While the Constitution does not directly refer to federalism, it does divide government power into national government, state government, and powers prohibited to government [see Figure 3-2 on p. 89]. National government power can be described as enumerated, implied, and inherent. Enumerated powers are found in the first seventeen clauses of Article I, Section 8. Implied powers come from the "necessary and proper" clause, the last clause of Article I, Section 8. Inherent powers arise out of the fact that governments have an inherent right to ensure their own survival. Under the supremacy clause, Article VI, Paragraph 2, federal laws are superior to all conflicting state and local laws [p. 91].

Reserved powers are powers given to state governments and come from the 10th Amendment, which states that powers not enumerated or denied are reserved to the states. An important state power is police power, which is the authority to legislate for the health, morals, safety, and welfare of the citizens of the states. Finally, the Constitution established relationships between states called horizontal federalism. These relationships are found in Article IV, Section 1, The Full Faith and Credit Clause; Article IV, Section 2, Privileges and Immunities; and Article IV, Section 2, Interstate Extradition. States may also set up interstate compacts if approved by Congress [p. 92].

National and state governments share some powers, like the power to tax. These shared powers are called concurrent powers [p. 90]. Powers denied to government are called prohibited powers, and deny powers to both national and state governments.

Defining Constitutional Powers The Early Years

To be effective over the centuries, the constitution had to be flexible. Two areas left open to interpretation by the Supreme Court were the "necessary and proper" clause and the commerce clauses. In the case of *McCulloch v. Maryland* (1819) Chief Justice John Marshall ruled that the "necessary and proper" clause of Article I, Section 8, embraced "all means which are appropriate to carry out" the legitimate ends of the Constitution [p. 93]. In *Gibbons v. Ogden* (1824) Chief Justice Marshall ruled that the power to regulate interstate commerce in Article I, Section 8, was an exclusive national power.

States' Rights and the Resort to Civil War

The Jacksonian era (1829-1837) created a climate that led most Southern states to attempt to nullify national laws and justify secession from the federal union [p. 96]. The defeat of the South in the Civil War ended the theory of nullification and secession. The war effort created a larger and more powerful national government, which, for the first time, imposed an income tax on its citizens.

The Continuing Dispute over the Division of Power

Although the outcome of the Civil War established the supremacy of the national government, the debate over the division of authority continued through the stages of dual federalism, cooperative federalism, and new federalism. In dual federalism, which faded in the 1930's, the state governments and national government are viewed as separate entities, like separate layers in a cake [p. 97].

Cooperative federalism, which was created to deal with the disaster of the depression, advocated cooperation between the state and national governments to solve problems, like merged layers in a marble cake [p. 98]. Picket-fence Federalism, created in the 1960's as another metaphor for cooperative federalism, added local government to the mix. This theory positions national, state, and local governments as the horizontal boards on a fence of vertical pickets that represent different policies. Each horizontal level of government works to the develop the policy represented by the picket.

Federal grants-in-aid [p. 99] illustrate how these different types of federalism work. The three major types of federal grants are: categorical grants-in-aid designed for specific state or local government programs or projects; matching funds, which require state and local governments to share the cost of the program; and equalization funds, which evaluate the relative wealth of the state or local entities.

New Federalism, labeled by President Nixon, advocates limiting the national government's power to regulate, and restoring power to state governments. Block grants implement the new federalism [p. 101]. These grants, which carry fewer restrictions than grants-in-aid, are federal programs that provide funding to state and local government for general functional areas (such as housing).

Trends in Federalism

An important argument for the new federalism contends that the national government has exceeded its constitutional authority, primarily through federal mandates [see Table 3-2 on p. 103]. A federal mandate is a requirement in federal legislation that forces states and local governments to comply with certain rules. As such, federal mandates have become a major barrier to returning authority to state government. In two recent Supreme Court decisions, the federal courts agreed with that argument [p. 105]. In the case of *United States v. Lopez* (1995), the Gun-Free School Zones Act of 1990, based on Congress' power under the commerce clause, was ruled unconstitutional. In *Printz v. United States* (1997), provisions of the Brady Handgun Violence Prevention Act of 1993, which required state employees to enforce these provisions, were ruled unconstitutional.

Competitive Federalism—An Alternate Model

Political scientist Thomas Dye has advocated a model of federalism in which state and local governments compete with one another to provide goods and services and attract "customers."

Federalism: Issues for the New Century

The new federalism has yet to become a reality because cooperative federalism created an entrenched national bureaucracy. The growth of state and local governments, however, may provide "laboratories" for the creation of experimental programs and policies that modify the current system.

KEY TERMS

block grants—p. 89

categorical grant-in-aid—p. 85

commerce clause—p. 80

concurrent powers—p. 75

confederate system—p. 70

cooperative federalism—p. 84

dual federalism—p. 82

elastic clause—p. 74

enumerated powers—p. 74

equalization—p. 85

federal mandate—p. 92

federal system—p. 70

horizontal federalism—p. 77

injunction—p. 80

matching funds—p. 85

necessary and proper clause—p. 74

new federalism—p. 88

nullification—p. 82

police power—p. 75

secession—p. 82

supremacy clause—p. 76

unitary system—p. 70

C D- RO M *AMERICA AT ODDS*

DRUG POLICY. The interactive module for Chapter 3 addresses governmental regulation of drugs. Government concern over drug usage was almost nonexistent in the 19th Century, and reflected a society under dual federalism with its limited scope for government. The Pure Food and Drug Act of 1906 was the first law to regulate the sale of drugs. This module contains interactive questions on the opposing issues of legalization versus criminalization of drugs, and the question of limiting the supply or demand of drugs. The chosen approach will determine whether the states or the national government will spearhead the anti-drug effort. A ten-question interactive multiple-choice quiz reinforces key points in the material.

PRACTICE EXAM

(Answers appear at the end of this chapter.)

Fill-in-the-Blank. Supply the missing word(s) or term(s) to complete the sentence.

1. A _____ system of government divides power between a central government and

    susidiary governments.

2. _____ powers derive from the U. S. status as a sovereign power among nations.

3. The Tenth Amendment establishes the _____ powers of the states.

4. The activities, problems, and policies that make up the relationships among states are referred to as

   _____ _____.

5. The _____ and _____ clause in the Constitution requires that states extend the

   same protections to the citizens of other states as they extend to their own citizens.

6. The issue in *McCulloch v. Maryland* was whether the national government has _____ powers.

7. President Reagan and congressional Republicans supported the development of _____ grants.

8. The doctrine that makes a distinction between federal and state spheres of governmental authority is

   referred to as _____ _____.

9. The goal of _____ _____ is to restore more power to state and local governments.

10. _____ _____ require state and local governments to comply with certain rules.

True/False. Circle the appropriate letter to indicate if the statement is true or false.
1. T   F   A unitary system of government is the easiest system to define.
2. T   F   The United States Constitution expressly designates a federal system of government.
3. T   F   The national government may deny the use of reserved powers to the states.
4. T   F   The Tenth Amendment provides for the reserved powers to the states.

5.   T   F   Most concurrent powers of the states are specifically stated in the Constitution.

6.   T   F   Under horizontal federalism, a state can set itself apart from the other states.

7.   T   F   Chief Justice John Marshall was a strong supporter of states' rights.

8.   T   F   The case of *McCulloch v. Maryland* (1819) set a precedent for a narrow interpretation of the implied powers of Congress.

9.   T   F   Dual federalism makes a distinction between federal and state spheres of authority.

10. T   F   The goal of new federalism is to restore more power to the state and local governments.

Multiple-Choice. Circle the correct response.

1.   The most popular way of ordering relations between a central government and its local units is by a

   a.   confederate system.

   b.   federal system.

   c.   unitary system.

   d.   constitutional system.

2.   If ultimate governmental authority rests in the hands of a central government, that is a

   a.   federal system.

   b.   confederate system.

   c.   unitary system.

   d.   theocratic system.

3.   A league of independent states, in which the central government holds only those powers expressly delegated to it, is a

   a.   federal system.

   b.   confederate system.

   c.   unitary system.

   d.   democratic system.

4.   Federalism appealed to the framers of the Constitution because it

   a.   allowed the states to control the process of government decision making.

   b.   retained state traditions and local power while it established a strong national government.

   c.   was acceptable to the British Parliament.

   d.   did not change the status quo.

5.   The essential argument in *Federalist Paper No. 10* is that

   a.   a unitary government is the best kind of government for a diverse society.

   b.   smaller political units are likely to be dominated by a single political group.

   c.   a unitary system of government is the most efficient.

   d.   only with a strong chief executive can the U.S. maintain its independence in world politics.

6. A special category of national powers that are not implied by the "necessary and proper" clause covers

    a. inherent powers.

    b. enumerated powers.

    c. extraordinary powers.

    d. elongated powers.

7. A resident of Kansas will be treated as an equal citizen in California because of the Constitution's

    a. privileges and immunities clause.

    b. full faith and credit clause.

    c. interstate commerce clause.

    d. extradition clause.

8. The issue in *McCulloch v. Maryland* was

    a. judiciary supremacy of the Supreme Court.

    b. the use of delegated power by the president.

    c. whether the commerce clause covered the regulation of shipping on the open seas.

    d. the use of implied powers by the national government.

9. Federal grants to state and local governments to cover specific programs and projects are referred to as

    a. block grants.

    b. revenue sharing.

    c. unfunded mandates.

    d. categorical grants-in-aid.

10. The goal of new federalism is to

    a. restore more power to state and local governments.

    b. restore more power to the national government.

    c. realign the relationship between states and their local units of government.

    d. make the national government more competitive in the world market.

11. Because of the supremacy clause the states cannot

    a. deny citizens of another state the same privileges they extend to their own citizens.

    b. use their reserved or concurrent powers to thwart national policies.

    c. discriminate against citizens from another state.

    d. tax their citizens beyond national governmental rates.

12. Picket-fence federalism added what element to the national and state governments?

    a. Interest groups

    b. Local government

    c. Multi-national corporations

    d. Political parties

13. In the cases of *Printz v. U.S.* and *U.S. v. Lopez*, the Supreme Court ruled that

    a. the national government exceeded its regulatory powers.

    b. the state government exceeded its reserved powers.

    c. the local government exceeded its police powers.

    d. both state and national government exceeded constitutional powers.

14. The concept of competitive federalism rests on

    a. competition between state and national government for power to regulate.

    b. competition between state and local governments for power to regulate.

    c. competition for customers in other countries by the national government.

    d. competition for customers by state and local government to provide services for citizens of other governments.

15. In the new century, new federalism advocates that significant "laboratories" for experimental programs be created by

    a. the national government.

    b. state and local governments.

    c. private foundations.

    d. multi-national corporations.

Short Essay Questions. Briefly address the major concepts raised by the following questions.

1. Discuss three ways of organizing relations between a central government and its local governmental units.

2. Identify and explain the division of powers between the national and state governments in the Constitution.

3. Trace and explain the debate over the division of powers between national and state government since the Civil War.

4. Discuss the latest trends in our federal system, including federal mandates, Supreme Court decisions, and competitive federalism.

ANSWERS TO THE PRACTICE EXAM

Fill-in-the-Blank.

1. federal [p. 86]

2. inherent [p. 90]

3. reserved [p. 90]

4. horizontal federalism [p. 92]

5. privileges and immunities [p. 92]

6. implied [p. 94]

7. block [p. 101]

8. dual federalism [p. 97]

9. new federalism [p. 101]

10. federal mandates [p. 103]

True/False.

1. T [p. 85]	3. F [p. 90]	5. F [p. 90]	7. F [p. 93]	9. T [p. 97]
2. F [p. 88]	4. T [p. 90]	6. F [p. 92]	8. F [p. 94]	10. T [p. 101]

Multiple-Choice.

1. c [p. 85]	4. b [p. 87]	7. a [p. 93]	10. a [p. 101]	13. a [p. 105]
2. c [p. 85]	5. b [p. 88]	8. d [p. 94]	11. b [p. 91]	14. d [p. 106]
3. b [p. 86]	6. a [p. 90]	9. d [p. 99]	12. b [p. 99	15. b [p. 107]

Short Essay Answers.

An adequate short answer consists of several paragraphs that discuss the concepts raised by the question. Always demonstrate your knowledge of the ideas by giving examples. The following represent major ideas that should be included in these short essays.

1. Discuss three ways of organizing relations between a central government and its local governmental units. Refer to Figure 3-1 on page 87 for a review of the different vehicles and how power flows in each.

    • Unitary system in which a centralized government gives some powers to local or subdivisonal governments [p. 85].

    • Confederate system in which a league of independent states grants specific powers to the central federal government [p. 86].

    • Federal system in which power is divided between a central government and regional or subdivisional governments [p. 86].

2. Identify and explain the division of powers between the national and state governments in the Constitution. Refer to Figure 3-2 on page 89 for an overview of selected constitutional powers.

    • National government powers

        ◊ Expressed or enumerated powers in Article 1, Section 8.

        ◊ Implied powers derived from the necessary and proper clause [p. 90].

    • Shared by national and state governments: concurrent powers [p. 90-91].

    • State powers: reserved powers derived from the 10th amendment to the Constitution [p. 90].

    • The supremacy clause places federal law over conflicting state and local law [p. 91].

3. Trace and explain the debate since the Civil War over the division of powers between national and state government.

    • Dual federalism is the system of government in which the state and national governments remain supreme within their own spheres [p. 97].

    • Cooperative federalism is the system in which the state and national governments cooperate in solving problems. Federal grants-in-aid implement cooperative federalism [p. 98-100].

- New federalism is the plan to limit the national government's regulatory power by restoring power to state governments. Block grants are a key tool in the creation of new federalism [p. 101-102].

4. Discuss the latest trends in our federal system, including federal mandates, Supreme Court decisions, and competitive federalism.

    - Federal mandates require state and local governments to comply with certain rules, and are a major barrier to new federalism. [See Figure 3-2 on p. 103 for major mandates from 1994-1998.]

    - *Printz v. U.S.* stuck down the provision of the Brady bill that required state employees to check the background of prospective handgun purchasers [p. 105].

    - The *Lopez* case held that the Gun-Free School Zones Act in 1990 exceeded Congress' authority under the commerce clause of the constitution [p. 105].

    - Competitive federalism is the concept that state and local governments should compete with one another to provide goods and services to "customers" for the best price [p. 106].

    - All of these trends except for federal mandates are moving our federal system away from a dominant national government and toward a decentralization of power among national, state, and local governments.

Chapter 4
Civil Liberties

CHAPTER SUMMARY

Civil Liberties and the Fear of Government.

As outlined in the Bill of Rights, civil liberties refer to individual rights that cannot by restrained by government actions. A few rights, like prohibiting *ex post facto* laws are found in Article I, Section 9, of the Constitution [p. 115].

The Nationalization of the Bill of Rights.

Most citizens are not aware that the Bill of Rights originally applied only to the national government. Incorporation theory holds that the protections of the Bill of Rights was applied to state governments by the 14th Amendment, ratified in 1868, under its due process clause. The Supreme Court has gradually, but not completely, accepted this theory. The first right to be incorporated was freedom of speech in the case of *Gitlow v. New York* (1925). See Table 4-1 on p. 116 for a list of cases incorporating various aspects of the Bill of Rights.

Freedom of Religion.

Opening with the words, "Congress shall make no law respecting an establishment of religion", the First Amendment to the Constitution begins with two basic principles of freedom of religion:

- the no establishment clause
- the free exercise of religion

The establishment clause or separation of church and state, as Thomas Jefferson called it, covers such conflicts as state and local aid to religion, school prayer, and teaching evolution versus creationism [p. 117]. In *Lemon v. Kurtzman* (1971) the Supreme Court ruled that direct state aid could not be used to subsidize religious instruction. This case created a three-part test for the no establishment clause. The *Engel v. Vitale* case (1962) ruled that school sponsored prayer was a violation of the no establishment clause. The *Edwards v. Aguillard* case (1987) ruled that teaching the biblical story of creation was a violation of the no establishment clause. In recent years, the Supreme Court seemed to be lowering the barrier between church and state. In 1995, in *Rosenberger v. University of Virginia*, the Court ruled that if the university funds various campus groups' newsletters, it must also fund a Christian newsletter.

The free exercise clause has usually focused on striking a balance between religious belief and religious practice. In *Oregon v. Smith* (1990), a case in which two Native-American drug counselors were fired for using the illegal drug peyote in their religious services, the court ruled that religious practices can be regulated [p. 123].

Freedom of Expression.

More than any other liberty, Americans probably exercise their right to freedom of expression the most. But this right cannot be used to justify saying any thing, any time, in any place. The Supreme Court has established some reasonable restrictions on free speech. The clear and present danger test from *Schenck v. U.S.* (1919) restricted speech that provokes a "clear and present danger" to public order. The bad-tendency rule from *Gitlow v. N.Y.* (1925) limited speech that might lead to some evil.

Prior restraint to regulate speech, that is, censorship, has usually been ruled unconstitutional by the Court [p. 124 and this freedom from censorship has protected individuals, newspapers, movies, and TV shows. In *New York Times v. U.S.* (1971), one of the most famous cases, the Supreme Court ruled that the New York Times had the right to publish information contained in the Pentagon Papers about the Vietnam War [p. 125]. The Court has also given protection to speech that uses symbols to express opposition to the government, as well as commercial speech contained in advertising. In a highly controversial case, *Texas v. Johnson* (1989), flag burning was given protection as symbolic speech [p. 126].

Clear examples of individuals using their freedom of speech to deny rights to others have not been considered constitutionally protected [p. 127-128]. These areas include obscenity, slander, fighting words, hecklers' veto, and hate speech. The Supreme Court in *Miller v. California* (1973) created a four-part list of requirements for determining obscenity. Slander and libel are wrongfully injuring a person's reputation. Slander is spoken; libel is written.

Freedom of the Press.

Freedom of the press is viewed as printed speech, an interpretation that applies freedom of expression to the press. Libel is the written defamation of a person's character, and is a major concern of the mass media today. The Supreme Court in *New York Times v. Sullivan* (1964) gave some protection to media by ruling that public figures who sue for libel must prove malice on the part of the media. This greater burden of proof for public figures allows for the criticism of public officials and discussions of differences of opinion without fear of lawsuits.

Another important issue for a free press is the conflict between the public's right to know, and the rights of individuals or the police in the criminal justice system. In *Gannett Company v. De Pasquale* (1979), the Supreme Court ruled that a judge could issue a gag order to protect a defendant from excessive news publicity that would prejudice a defendant's right to a fair trial [p. 129]. The Court ruled in *Zucher v. Stanford* (1978) that news reporters do not have the right of confidentiality if law enforcement needs information for criminal prosecution [p. 130].

The broadcast media, radio, TV, and movies, generally have more restrictions than print media because of Federal Communication Commission regulations. The equal time rule, personal attack rule, and fairness doctrine provide for all broadcast media to try to present both sides of an issue [p. 131].

Chapter 4   Civil Liberties

The Right to Assemble and to Petition the Government.

These rights often involve free speech since few demonstrations involve silent protests. The key issue is how to balance this right with the necessity for public officials to maintain public order and control traffic. The Supreme Court, in *Smith v. Collin* (1978), upheld the right of Nazis to march in the Chicago area when they had been denied a parade permit by the city of Skokie, Illinois [p. 132].

More Liberties under Scrutiny: Matters of Privacy.

The right to privacy has no explicit mention in the Constitution. It stems from the Supreme Court case *Griswold v. Connecticut* (1965). The Court ruled that right to privacy stems from "penumbras" in the First, Third, Fourth, Fifth, and Ninth Amendments in the Bill of Rights. The information age, and the vast amount of information collected on the average citizen, has brought concern with privacy rights to the forefront of the public agenda.

The first major application of privacy rights was *Roe v. Wade* (1973), in which the Supreme Court accepted the argument that laws against abortion violate a woman's right to privacy [p. 133]. This decision has created, probably the most divisive public policy issue in America, even though later Court decisions placed restrictions on abortion rights [p. 134-135].

A second major application of right to privacy is the right to die. The New Jersey Supreme Court in the *Quinlan* case in 1976 established this principle, and the U.S. Supreme Court modified it in *Cruzan v. Director, Missouri Department of Health* (1990). The Cruzan case has led to the creation of "living wills" and other documents to safeguard the right to die. In the related issue of assisted suicide, which only Oregon allows, the Court has left the right to state government [p. 136].

The Great Balancing Act: The Rights of the Accused versus the Rights of Society.

The Constitution attempts to balance the rights of individuals against the rights of society, particulary the rights of those accused of criminal offenses. The Fourth, Fifth, Sixth, and Eighth Amendments deal with the rights of criminal defendants. [See a complete listing of these rights on p. 137-138.]

During the 1960's, the Supreme Court greatly expanded the rights of the accused. In 1963, *Gideon v. Wainwright* granted a poor defendant the right to an attorney, in most cases. In 1966, *Miranda v. Arizona* required police to inform an individual of his or her constitutional rights prior to questioning. Recent Court decisions have placed some restrictions on the Miranda ruling in a continuing effort to find the right balance between individual, and societal rights [p. 139].

The exclusionary rule, which prohibited the admission of illegally obtained evidence during a trial, was applied to federal court in 1914. The concept was first applied to state courts in the case of *Mapp v. Ohio* (1961). [Refer back to Table 4-1 on p. 116 for incorporation cases.] Recent Court decisions have provided some discretion for police officers who are acting in "good faith" [p. 140].

Furman v. Georgia that the death penalty was random and arbitrary. This case was based on the existing state laws of the death penalty, which have been changed, and today exist in 38 states [p. 141]. The Court ruled in *Stanford v. Kentucky* (1989) that mentally retarded persons may be executed for murder, and in *McClesky v. Kemp* (1987) that statistical evidence does not prove racial bias in the death penalty [p. 142].

Civil Liberties: Issues for the New Century.

The growth of the Internet will produce new challenges in defining free expression rights. The exercise of religious rights, particularly in institutions like schools, continues to stir controversy. The protection of privacy rights in our online culture, and the issues of abortion and the right to die continue to defy solutions. Crime will continue to be a problem as our society looks for new ways to balance the rights of the accused with the rights of us all [p. 143].

KEY TERMS

actual malice—p. 129

bad-tendency—p. 124

civil liberties—p. 115

clear and present danger—p. 124

establishment clause—p. 117

exclusionary rule—p. 139

fairness doctrine—p. 131

fighting words—p. 127

free exercise clause—p. 122

incorporation theory—p. 116

libel—p. 128

prior restraint—p. 124

public figures—p. 129

slander—p. 127

symbolic speech—p. 126

writ of *habeas corpus*—p. 138

C D- RO M *AMERICA AT ODDS*

THE RIGHT TO DIE. The interactive module for Chapter 4 deals with the topic of the individual's right to die under the concept of the Right of Privacy. In 1976, the New Jersey Supreme Court ruled in the Quinlan case that the right to privacy includes the right of a patient to refuse treatment, and to exercise that right through a family member. The *Cruzan v. Director, Missouri Department of Health* (1990) case of the U.S. Supreme Court decided that "clear and convincing evidence" must be available to stop treatment. These cases have created laws allowing "living wills" to provide this evidence. The module also looks at the pros and cons of assisted suicide. A ten-question interactive multiple-choice quiz allows you to reinforce key points in the material.

PRACTICE EXAM

(Answers appear at the end of this chapter.)

Fill-in-the-Blank. Supply the missing word(s) or term(s) to complete the sentence.

1. _____ _____ restrain a government's actions against individuals.

2. It was not until the _____ Amendment was ratified that our Constitution explicitly guaranteed due process of law to everyone.

3. The *Lemon* Test defines the ____ _____ _____ in freedom of religion.

4. According to the _____ _____ rule, speech or other First Amendment freedoms may be curtailed if such expression might lead to some evil.

5. Burning the American flag as part of a peaceful protest is considered _____ expressive conduct.

6. For slander to be judged defamation of character there must be a _____ witness.

7. Only when a statement is made with _____ _____ can a public official receive damages for libel.

8. In the 1990s, the most controversial aspect of the right to die is _____ assisted suicide.

9. The _____, _____, _____, and _____ Amendments deal with the rights of criminal defendants.

10. The use of illegally seized evidence is prohibited in a trial because of the _____ rule.

True/False. Circle the appropriate letter to indicate if the statement is true or false.

1. T   F   The prohibition against *ex post facto* laws is one of the few specific limits on government power found in the main text of the constitution.

2. T   F   As originally presented, the Bill of Rights limited only the powers of the states, not the national government.

3. T   F   Most of the guarantees in the Bill of Rights now apply to the fifty states.

4. T   F   The use of state aid to private religious schools has been accepted by the Supreme Court.

5. T   F   For the most part, American are very limited in their freedom to criticize public officials.

6. T   F   The federal courts have not extended constitutional protections of free speech to pornography, which is considered obscene.

7. T   F   Gag orders restrict the publication of news about a trial in progress or a pretrial hearing.

8. T   F   The right of privacy is explicitly guaranteed in the Bill of Rights.

9. T   F   The *Webster* and *Planned Parenthood* decisions have made access to legal abortions easier.

10. T   F   The United States has one of the highest violent crime rates in the world.

Multiple-Choice. Circle the correct response.

1. When we speak of civil liberties, we are referring to limitations on government as outlined in the
    a. Declaration of Independence.
    b. Magna Carta.
    c. Articles of Confederation.
    d. Bill of Rights.

2. The view that most of the protections of the Bill of Rights are included under the Fourteenth Amendment's protection against state government is called the
    a. inclusionary theory.
    b. nullification theory.
    c. necessary and proper theory.
    d. incorporation theory.

3. The three-part Lemon test concerns the issue of
    a. symbolic speech.
    b. state aid to church-related schools.
    c. presentation of evidence before a grand jury.
    d. the right-to-die.

4. The First Amendment does not prevent the government from curtailing religious practices that

    a. work against public policy and the public welfare.

    b. infringe on citizen's sensitivities.

    c. are defined by media as "cult" religions.

    d. are a willful violation of the Pledge of Allegiance at public school.

5. According to the "clear and present danger" test

    a. a speech must be unclear as to its intent for it to be ruled unconstitutional.

    b. the action called for must be constitutionally "vague" in order to be ruled unconstitutional.

    c. free speech can be curbed if such speech causes a condition that Congress has the power to prevent.

    d. Free speech may not be curbed, because speech alone cannot bring about action.

6. The burning of an American flag in a peaceful protest is an example of

    a. a violation of the Constitution.

    b. a protected action under the clear and present danger concept.

    c. a protected action under the symbolic speech concept.

    d. an issue not yet decided by the Supreme Court.

7. Paid advertising can be constitutionally protected as a form of

    a. commercial speech.

    b. symbolic speech.

    c. exempted speech.

    d. private speech.

8. The *Miller v. California* case created a list of requirements that apply to

    a. abortion.

    b. religious freedom.

    c. obscenity.

    d. libel.

9. Individuals using "fighting words" or exercising a "heckler's veto"

    a. are exercising constitutionally protected forms of speech.

    b. are exercising constitutionally protected forms of freedom of religion.

    c. are not within the bounds of constitutional protection.

    d. are in a vague area that the federal courts have not ruled on.

10. Public officials may sue for libel if they can prove the statement

    a. was false.

    b. hurt the official's reputation.

    c. hurt the official's feelings.

    d. was made with actual malice.

11. Gag orders are

    a.   designed to eliminate illegal speech.

    b.   designed to eliminate unlawful assembly.

    c.   restrictions on the publication of news concerning pretrial hearing or trials in progress.

    d.   part of the controversy over the death penalty.

12. The *Roe v. Wade* case decided the abortion issue on the basis of

    a.   freedom of religion.

    b.   freedom of speech.

    c.   right to privacy.

    d.   the incorporation theory.

13. The exclusionary rule prohibits

    a.   defendants from testifying in their own behalf.

    b.   improperly obtained evidence from being used by prosecutors.

    c.   a spouse from testifying in a criminal case.

    d.   the defense counsel from having access to the prosecution's evidence.

14. Historically, "cruel and unusual" punishment has referred to punishments

    a.   that were not acceptable to society.

    b.   for crimes that were classified as unusually cruel.

    c.   that were more serious than the crime.

    d.   for political crimes.

15. A recent issue involving the death penalty debate has concerned the issue of

    a.   the mandatory death sentence without an appeal.

    b.   the execution of mentally retarded persons.

    c.   the method of execution.

    d.   the right to an attorney in death penalty cases.

Short Essay Questions. Briefly address the major concepts raised by the following questions.

1. Explain the historical context for the importance of the Bill of Rights within the Constitution.

2. Identify and explain the two concepts of freedom of religion contained in the First Amendment.

3. Discuss the important principles established by the Supreme Court for freedom of speech and press.

4. Outline and discuss the right of individuals accused of a crime.

ANSWERS TO THE PRACTICE EXAM

Fill-in-the-Blank..

1. Civil Liberties [p. 115]
2. Fourteenth [p. 116]
3. no establishment clause [p. 117]
4. bad-tendency[p. 124]
5. symbolic [p. 126]

6. third [p. 127]
7. actual malice [p. 129]
8. physican [p. 137]
9. Fourth, Fifth, Sixth, Eighth [p. 137]
10. exclusionary [p. 139]

True/False.

1.	T [p. 115]	3.	T [p. 116]	5.	F [p. 123]	7.	T [p. 129]	9.	F [p. 135]
2.	F [p. 115]	4.	F [p. 118]	6.	T [p. 92]	8.	F [p. 132]	10.	T [p. 137]

Multiple Choice.

1. d [p. 115]	4. a [p. 122]	7. a [p. 126]	10. d [p. 129]	13. b [p. 139]
2. d [p. 116]	5. c [p. 124]	8. c [p. 127]	11. c [p. 129]	14. c [p. 140]
3. b [p. 118]	6. c [p. 126]	9. c [p. 128]	12. c [p. 133]	15. b [p. 142]

Short Essay Answers.

An adequate short answer consists of several paragraphs that address the concepts raisedby the question. Always demonstrate your knowledge of the ideas by giving examples. The following represent major ideas that should be included in these short essays.

1. Explain the historical context for the importance of the Bill of Rights within the Constitution.
   - Few specific restrictions on government were contained in the constitution [p. 115-116].
   - The Bill of Rights did not apply to state governments.
   - The Fourteenth Amendment guaranteed and applied the civil liberties of the Constitution to the states, which is called incorporation.
   - Only gradually on a case-by-case basis, but never completely, has the Supreme Court accepted incorporation. See Table 4-1 for a list of cases incorporating different constitutional rights.
2. Identify and explain the two concepts of freedom of religion contained in the First Amendment.
   - The no establishment clause prohibits official government support of religion [p. 117-121].
     ◊ *Lemon v. Kurtzman* (1971) creates a three-part test of this concept.
     ◊ *Engle v. Vitale* (1962) ruled that official prayer in public school is unconstitutional.
     ◊ Teaching of evolution cannot be banned and the Bible story of creation cannot be taught.
   - The free exercise of religion shall not be prohibited [p. 122-123].

◊ Religious beliefs are absolute but religious practices that work against public policy and public welfare may be restricted.

◊ *Oregon v. Smith* (1990) ruled that Native Americans could be denied unemployment benefits when fired from a state job for using peyote in their religious services.

◊ Congress passed the Religious Freedom Restoration Act (RFRA) in 1993 to require all levels of government to "accommodate religious conduct".

◊ *City of Boerne v. Flores* (1997) ruled the RFRA law unconstitutional.

3. Discuss the important principles established by the Supreme Court for freedom of speech and press.

• Freedom of speech has never been considered absolute; some restrictions are permitted p. 124-128.

◊ *Schenck v. U.S.* (1919) held that Congress has the constitutional right to prevent speech that provokes a "clear and present danger."

◊ *Gitlow v. New York* (1925) held that expression leading to some "evil" is not protected.

◊ However, in the *New York Times v. U.S.* (1971), the Supreme Court ruled that prior restraint or censorship is unconstitutional.

• Symbolic speech and commercial speech have received constitutional protection. *Texas v. Johnson* (1989), ruled that burning an American flag in a peaceful protest is protected as symbolic speech.

• Some speech has never been constitutionally protected.

◊ Obscenity, defined by *Miller v. California* (1973), is not protected.

◊ Slander, the public uttering of a false statement that harms a person's reputation, is not protected.

◊ Fighting words, heckler's veto, and hate speech, which are examples of using speech to prevent others from exercising their rights, are not protected.

• Freedom of the press is viewed as printed speech; many of the same concepts apply [p. 128-131].

◊ Libel is the written defamation of a person's reputation, but the press has some limited protection from charges of libel.

◊ *The New York Times v. Sullivan* (1964) created the concept of a public figure who, in order to sue for libel, must prove actual malice on the part of media.

◊ Another significant free press issue is conflict between free press and a criminal suspect's right to a fair trial. *Gannett Company v. De Pasquale* (1979) allowed judges to issue gag orders to restrict the publication of news about pretrial hearings or trials in progress.

◊ The confidentiality of news sources was not constitutionally protected in *Zurcher v. Stanford Daily* (1978).

• Broadcast media has generally not been protected in the same manner as published materials. The Federal Communication Commission (FCC) has created guidelines such as the equal time rule, the personal attack rule, and the fairness doctrine.

4. Outline and discuss the rights of an individual accused of a crime [p. 137-142].

- In the Bill of Rights, the Fourth, Fifth, Sixth, and Eighth Amendments deal with rights of criminal defendants. The process is divided into three parts.
    ◊ Limits on the conduct of police officers and prosecutors
    ◊ Defendant's pretrial rights
    ◊ Trial rights
- The Fourth Amendment protects against an unreasonable search and seizure of evidence. The exclusionary rule prevented this evidence from being admitted at the trial in a federal case. This concept was not incorporated, that is applied to state cases, until the *Mapp v. Ohio* case in 1961.
- The Fifth Amendment provides for the right to remain silent, to be informed of the charges, and the right to legal counsel. In *Miranda v. Arizona* (1966), the Supreme Court ruled that upon questioning, a suspect must be informed of his or her rights.
- The Sixth Amendment provides for legal counsel during a trial, even if the defendant cannot afford one. In *Betts v. Brady* (1942), this concept was applied only to capital cases. In 1963, the *Gideon v. Wainwright* case applied the right to legal counsel to anyone accused of a felony offense.
- The Eighth Amendment protects against "cruel and unusual" punishment. Most of the debate on this issue has centered around the death penalty. In 1972, the Supreme Court ruled in *Furman v. Georgia* that the death penalty was random and arbitrary. The court invited states to pass death penalty laws that were more precise, and therefore, constitutional. Most states have done so. Today, one finds an increasing use of the death penalty. In 1989, the Supreme Court ruled in *Penry v. Lynaugh* that mentally retarded persons could be executed, and in *Stanford v. Kentucky,* that defendants as young as sixteen could be executed.

Chapter 5
Civil Rights: Equal Protection

CHAPTER SUMMARY

Civil Rights are the rights of all Americans to equal treatment under law, as provided in the Fourteenth Amendment to the Constitution.

African Americans and the Consequences of Slavery in the United States

Before 1863, the Constitution protected slavery. In *Dred Scott v. Sanford* (1857), the Supreme Court had upheld the constitutionality of slavery by ruling that slaves were not citizens of the United States [p. 152]. President Lincoln's Emancipation Proclamation in 1863, and the passage of the 13th, 14th, and 15th Amendments to the Constitution ended constitutional inequality.

From 1865-1875, to protect African-American rights from being violated by state government, rhe Republican-controlled Congress passed several Civil Rights Acts [p. 153]. But because the Supreme Court ruled these acts unconstitutional, they were largely ineffective. The most significant of these decisions was *Plessy v. Ferguson* (1896), which created the doctrine of separate-but-equal and led to racial segregation, particularly in the South. When federal troops that occupied the South were withdrawn in 1877, the Southern states restricted African-Americans' right to vote by imposing a number of laws, such as, the grandfather clause, poll taxes, and literacy tests. The white primary law was finally ruled unconstitutional in the 1944 case of *Smith v. Allwright*. P. 155.

The end to the separate-but-equal doctrine, and racial segregation began in the 1930s with a series of lawsuits to admit African Americans to graduate and professional schools. These lawsuits culminated in the unanimous Supreme Court decision in *Brown v. Board of Education of Topeka* in 1954, which ruled that public school segregation of the races violates the equal protection clause of the 14th Amendment [p. 156]. In reaction to this decision, state governments sought loopholes in the decision and society witnessed a tremendous increase in private, often religion-based schools. The early attempts to integrate schools often relied on court-ordered busing of students across neighborhoods. Recently, the federal courts have returned authority to local school officials, as in *Missouri v. Jenkins* (1995), which allowed Missouri to stop financing a magnet school for racial integration [p. 158].

The Civil Rights Movement

The *Brown* decision was a moral victory, but did little to change the underlying structure of segregation. In 1955, an African-American woman, Rosa Parks, refused to give up her seat on the bus to a white man. She was arrested and fined. Thus began the civil rights protests that would eventually end racial segregation. Martin Luther King, Jr., a Baptist minister, organized a year-long boycott of the Montgomery, Alabama bus line, the success of which propelled King to national leadership of the civilrights movement. The culmination of the movement came in 1963, when intending to influence civil rights legislation then pending in Congress, Dr. King led a march on Washington D.C. and gave his famous "I have a dream" speech [p. 160-162].

Modern Civil Rights Legislation

In passing the Civil Rights Act of 1964, Congress had created the most far-reaching bill on civil rights in modern times. The Act demolished discrimination in all areas, except housing, which was covered in the Civil Rights Act of 1968 [see p. 163 for the major provisions of the Act]. Congress followed up the 1964 Act with the Voting Rights Act of 1965, which eliminated discriminatory voter-registration laws and authorized federal officials to register voters, primarily in the South. Subsequent amendments to the Voting Rights Act granted protections, such as bilingual ballots, to other minorities [p. 165].

Melting Pot or Multicultural Mix?

The concept of the melting pot in American society described the idea that immigrants could best succeed by adopting the language and political values of the dominate culture. Questionning the validity of this concept, many people today think that American society should be seen as a multicultural country. See the critical perspective debate on this issue [p. 168-169]. Also see this topic's interactive modules on the *America at Odds* CD ROM.

Women's Struggle for Equal Rights

Women first became involved politically in the abolition of slavery movement. From this effort, Lucretia Mott and Elizabeth Cady Stanton organized the first women's rights convention in 1848 [p. 167]. The 1870 campaign to ratify the 15th Amendment, which gave voting rights to African-American men, split the women's suffrage movement. But women successfully campaigned for passage of the 19th Amendment, which enfranchised women and was ratified in 1920 [p. 170].

After achieving the right to vote, women engaged in little political activity until the 1960s, when the feminist movement called for political, economic, and social equality for women. The feminist movement attempted to obtain the ratification of an Equal Rights Amendment in the 1970s, but the necessary 38 states failed to ratify [p. 171]. After this defeat, the women's movement began to work for women's increased representation in government. Political Action Committees, PACs, were created to fund women candidates. The largest of these PACs is EMILY's list, which stands for "Early Money Is Like Yeast—It Makes the Dough Rise" [p. 173].

Political Leadership by Women

Although no major political party has nominated a woman for president, women have run for the vice-presidency and serve as members of the cabinet and the Supreme Court. Women have been elected governors of major states, mayors of large cities, and about 22% are state legislators. The number of women elected, however, remains low compared to their participation as voters [see Table 5-2 p. 174].

Gender-Based Discrimination in the Workplace

Title VII of the Civil Rights Act of 1964 prohibited gender discrimination in employment, including sexual harassment. In 1991, it became apparent that these laws were not being vigorously enforced when Anita Hill charged Supreme Court nominee Clarence Thomas with sexual harassment. This publicity resulted in an increasing number of court cases dealing with sexual harassment. Supreme Court cases like *Faragher v. City of Boca Raton* (1998), and *Burlington Industries v. Ellerth* (1998), ruled that employers and employees were libel for sexual harassment if they did not exercise reasonable care to prevent and correct promptly any sexually harassing behavior [p. 176]. In 1994, Paula Jones brought a lawsuit against President Clinton, accusing the president of sexually harassing her when he was governor of Arkansas. Although this case was dismissed, it led Special Prosecutor, Kenneth Starr to submit materials to Congress, alleging impeachable offenses derived from President Clinton's relationship with Monica Lewinsky [p. 176-177].

Another important issue for women in the workplace has been wage discrimination. Although the Equal Pay Act of 1963 was designed to provide for equal pay, a woman earns about seventy-eight cents for every dollar earned by a man. Some of the key reasons for this are the low pay for jobs traditionally held by women (such as child care), and the corporate "glass ceiling" that prevents women from reaching the highest executive positions in business [p. 178-179].

Civil Rights-Equal Protection: Issues for the New Century

While African Americans, minorities, and women have made major gains since 1950, they remain under-represented in national politics and participation. The debate over the melting pot of cultures versus ethnic separatism or multiculturalism will continue. The role of women in the workplace and equal pay issues will continue to be a focus of national domestic policy [p. 179].

KEY TERMS

busing—157

civil rights—151

comparable worth—178

de facto segregation—157

de jure segregation—157

feminism—171

gender discrimination—174

Grandfather Clause—155

literacy test—155

poll tax—155

separate-but-equal—155

sexual harassment—175

suffrage—169

white primary—155

C D-RO M *AMERICA AT ODDS*

ENGLISH ONLY. The module for Chapter 5 deals with whether we should make English the official language of the United States. Interactive questions encourage the reader to explore the idea of a melting pot, in which immigrants assimilate the language and values of the dominate culture, versus multiculturalism, in which immigrants retain their distinct cultural identities and languages. Hear two members of Congress, John Linder of Georgia, and Anthony Beilenson of California, debate the English-only issue, and examine provisions of the English Language Empowerment Act. A ten-question interactive multiple-choice quiz reinforces key points in the material.

PRACTICE EXAM

(Answers appear at the end of this chapter.)

Fill-in-the-Blank. Supply the missing word(s) or term(s) to complete the sentence.

1. In _____ v. _____, the Supreme Court confirmed the

    constitutionality of slavery

2. The constitutional principle that permitted racial segregation was called the _____ _____

    _____ _____.

3. The obvious solution to both *de facto* and *de jure* segregation of schools was _____.

4. Martin Luther King Jr.'s philosophy of _____ included such tactics as

    demonstrations and marches.

5. The _____ _____ _____ of 1964 was the most far-reaching civil rights bill in modern times.

6. The _____ _____ _____ of 1965 outlawed discriminatory voter-registration tests.

7. The theory that immigrants should adopt the language and political values of the dominant culture is

    called the _____ _____ _____.

8. By the year 2010, _____ will be the largest minority group in the United States.

9. The largest Political Action Committee for women candidates is called _____ list.

10. Barriers faced by women in the corporate world are referred to as the _____ _____.

True/False. Circle the appropriate letter to indicate if the statement is true or false.

1. T   F   The case of *Plessy v. Ferguson* created the separate-but-equal doctrine.
2. T   F   The Reconstruction statutes after the Civil War helped to secure civil rights for African-
            Americans equal to those of whites.
3. T   F   Concentrations of minorities in defined geographic locations results in *de facto* segregation.
4. T   F   The era of civil rights protests in the mid 1950s began with the boycott of public bus
            transportation in Montgomery, Alabama.
5. T   F   The white primary was used in southern states to deny African-Americans the right to vote.
6. T   F   African-Americans increased their political participation as a direct result of the Civil Rights
            Act of 1964.
7. T   F   *E pluribus unum*, Latin for "one out of many", is a slogan supporting multiculturalism.
8. T   F   During the national debate over the ratification of the ERA, a women's countermovement to
            feminism emerged.
9. T   F   No woman has ever held the office of Secretary of State in the President's cabinet.
10. T   F   Gender discrimination was prohibited by the Civil Rights Act of 1964.

Multiple-Choice. Circle the correct response.

1. The *Dred Scott* case
    a.   freed the slaves in the South.
    b.   contributed to a more peaceful resolution of the slavery issue.
    c.   contributed to making the Civil War inevitable.
    d.   provided full and equal citizenship for all African Americans.

2.   The reconstruction statutes had the effect of

   a.   securing equality for African Americans in their civil rights.

   b.   doing little to secure equality for African Americans in their civil rights.

   c.   restructuring society to provide for greater equality of opportunity.

   d.   setting the stage for the Civil War.

3.   The effect of *Plessy v. Ferguson* on racial segregation was to establish a

   a.   "clear and present danger" principle to further integration.

   b.   pattern to outlaw segregation in the South.

   c.   pattern for racial integration throughout the country.

   d.   constitutional cornerstone of racial discrimination throughout the country.

4.   An unintended effect of the Supreme Court's direction of "all deliberate speed" toward achieving integation in public education was that it

   a.   allowed some jurisdictions to integrate too quickly thereby causing confusion.

   b.   provided the pattern for complete integration of public education.

   c.   was used as a loophole by some jurisdictions to stall efforts toward integration.

   d.   created an influx of rural students attending urban schools.

5.   *De facto* segregation of school districts can come about through

   a.   residential concentration of minorities in defined geographical locations.

   b.   school boards drawing boundary lines to include only certain minority groups.

   c.   Supreme Court edicts.

   d.   a program of forced busing across district lines.

6.   Recent Supreme Court decisions on busing to integrate public schools have emphasized

   a.   more busing to fully integrate schools.

   b.   spending more money to attract minority students without busing.

   c.   stronger court controls over local schools.

   d.   restoring more control to local schools.

7.   Discrimination in most housing was forbidden by the

   a.   Civil Rights Act of 1964.

   b.   Civil Rights Act of 1968.

   c.   Voting Rights Act of 1965.

   d.   Equal Housing Act of 1965.

8. The "Rainbow Coalition" of Jesse Jackson was

    a. a group of conservationists organized to protect the national wetlands.

    b. the remnants of the Green Peace Movement.

    c. a campaign strategy to bring together women, minorities, and other underrepresented groups.

    d. a campaign slogan to identify the "traditional American" culture.

9. In terms if the women's movement in the U.S., the anti-slavery movement had the effect of

    a. retarding organized political action by women.

    b. enslaving women and creating a secondary status for them.

    c. creating the first political cause in which women could become actively engaged.

    d. allowing women to become the dominant force in this movement.

10. The first woman appointed to a president's cabinet was

    a. Sandra Day O'Connor.

    b. Susan B. Anthony.

    c. Francis Perkins.

    d. Jeannette Rankin.

11. Today, the overall national turnout of women voters is

    a. higher than that of male voters.

    b. much less because politics is considered to be a male activity.

    c. slightly less than that of male voters.

    d. about the same as elderly voters.

12. Sexual harassment of women in the workplace is

    a. no longer prohibited by statute.

    b. prohibited by Title VII of the Civil Rights Act of 1964.

    c. considered "protective" legislation which the Supreme Court has ruled unconstitutional.

    d. considered a form of reverse discrimination against men.

13. The Equal Pay Act of 1963 has

    a. never been enforced.

    b. only applied when women and men do exactly the same job.

    c. only applied to comparable worth situations.

    d. totally equalized pay between women and men.

14. The comparable worth doctrine attempts to redress the effects of traditional "women's work"

    a. by redefining what constitutes "women's work".

    b. by making all work pay at the same rate.

    c. by creating flex-time as a national standard.

    d. by taking into account skill, effort, and responsibility in determining pay.

15. The "glass ceiling" refers to

    a. subtle barriers that prevent women from being promoted to top positions in corporations.

    b. corporate espionage.

    c. reverse discrimination against men.

    d. national laws designed to protect women from wage discrimination.

Short Essay Questions. Briefly address the major concepts raised by the following questions.

1. Explain the impact on education of the Supreme Court's decision in *Brown v. Board of Education of Topeka,* and discuss what new problems the decision fostered.

2. Discuss the key events in the Civil Rights Movement that led to passage of the 1964 Civil Rights Act.

3. Discuss the provisions of the Voting Rights Act of 1965. What impact has this had on political participation among minority voters in the United States?

4. Explain the major issues of gender discrimination in the workplace.

ANSWERS TO THE PRACTICE EXAM

Fill-in-the-Blank..

1. *Dred Scott v. Sanford* [p. 152]
2. separate-but-equal doctrine [p. 155]
3. busing [p. 157]
4. nonviolence [p. 160]
5. Civil Rights Act [p. 162]
6. Voting Rights Act [p. 164]
7. the Melting Pot [p. 166]
8. Hispanics [p. 167]
9. Emily's [p. 173]
10. glass ceiling [p. 179]

True/False.

1. T [p. 155]	3. T [p. 157]	5. T [p. 155]	7. F [p. 166]	9. F [p. 174]
2. F [p. 154]	4. T [p. 159]	6. F [p. 163]	8. T [p. 171]	10. T [p. 174]

Multiple Choice.

1. c [p.152]	4. c [p. 156]	7. b [p. 163]	10. c [p. 173]	13. b [p. 178]
2. b [p. 154]	5. a [p.157]	8. c [p. 167]	11. a [p. 174]	14. d [p. 178]
3. d [p. 155]	6. d [p. 158]	9. c [p. 167]	12. b [p. 175]	15. a [p. 179]

Short Essay Answers

An adequate short answer consists of several paragraphs that relate to concepts raised by the question. Always demonstrate yourknowledge of the ideas by giving examples. The following represent major ideas that should be included in these short essays.

1.   Explain the impact on education of the Supreme Court's decision in *Brown v. Board of Education of Topeka* and discuss what new problems the decision fostered [p. 156-157].

   •   The concept of separate-but-equal from *Plessy v. Ferguson* was overturned.

   •   The order to implement "with all deliberate speed" was used as a loophole by state officials to slow the pace of integration of schools.

   •   School integration in Little Rock, Arkansas, was blocked by use of the state's National Guard.

   •   President Eisenhower federalized the Arkansas National guard and integrated schools in Little Rock.

   •   *De Jure* segregation is illegal under the Brown decision.

   •   *De Facto* segregation because of housing patterns is dealt with by busing to achieve integration.

2.   Discuss the key events in the Civil Rights Movement that led to the passage of the 1964 Civil Rights Act [p. 159-162].

   •   Rosa Parks refuses to move to the back of the bus, the "colored" section in Montgomery, Alabama.

   •   Martin Luther King, Jr leads a year-long African-American boycott of the Montgomery bus line.

   •   The Southern Christian Leadership Conference is formed.

   •   A series of nonviolent sit-ins, protests, demonstrations, and marches are held.

   •   Dr. King is arrested in Birmingham, Alabama, during a protest in which police use dogs and cattle prods on the demonstrators.

   •   Media coverage of these events has a profound effect on public opinion.

   •   Dr. King organizes a march on Washington, D.C., and delivers his famous "I have a Dream" speech, which is televised to millions.

3.   Discuss the provisions of the Voting Rights Act of 1965. How did this law influence the political participation of minority voters in the United States [p. 164-165]?

   •   Provision One outlawed the discriminatory voter-registration test.

   •   Provision Two authorized federal registration of voters and federally administered voting procedures.

   •   African-American registration and voting increased dramatically.

   •   More African Americans became prominent in national politics.

   •   Hispanic registration and voting increased dramatically.

   •   Bilingual ballots were authorized.

4. Explain the major issues of gender discrimination in the workplace.
    *   Title VII of the Civil Rights Act of 1964 prohibits gender discrimination in the workplace.
    *   One major issue is sexual harassment.
        ◊   Sexual harassment has been extended to the employer who does nothing to stop sexual harassment by and employee through court decisions in *Faragher v. City of Boca Raton* (1998), and *Burlington Industries v. Ellerth* (1998).
        ◊   Paula Jones sued President Clinton for sexual harassment in *Jones v. Clinton* (1994).
    *   Second major issue is wage discrimination.
        ◊   The Equal Pay Act of 1963 prohibits unequal pay for men and women doing the same job.
        ◊   Comparable worth is the concept that takes into account skill, effort, and responsibility to determine pay, because traditional "women's" jobs pay less than traditional "men's" jobs.
        ◊   Women have a harder time getting high corporate positions because of the "glass ceiling".

Chapter 6
Civil Rights: Beyond Equal Protection

CHAPTER SUMMARY

Affirmative Action

Although granted equality by the Civil Rights Act of 1964, past discrimination often meant that minority groups and women lacked the education and skills to compete for educational admissions and jobs. In 1965, the government tried to remedy this situation by creating Affirmative Action. Affirmative Action is a policy to give special consideration to traditionally disadvantaged groups in an effort to overcome the contemporary effects of past discrimination. This policy ran into serious problems in 1978 in the Supreme Court case of *Regents of the University of California v. Bakke*, which involved admission policies at UC-Davis Medical School. Alan Bakke argued that the affirmative action admission policy requiring a racial quota was reverse discrimination against those who do not have minority status. The Supreme Court agreed. In *Firefighters Local Union No. 1784 v. Stotts*, the Court ruled that affirmative action could not overrule the seniority principle in deciding layoffs [p. 188]. Congress attempted to clarify the concepts involved by passing the Civil Rights Act of 1991. The controversy continued in the 1990s, and in *Hopwood v. State of Texas* (1996), the Supreme Court ruled that any use of race to give an admission to law school was unconstitutional. Also in 1996, Proposition 209 was passed by the voters of California and ended all state-sponsored affirmative action programs [p. 190]. Majority public opinion still seems to favor affirmative action programs, because it is apparent that not only do the effects of discrimination continue today, but discrimination itself continues as well.

Bilingual Education

The recent rise in immigration to this country has created an educational dilemma about how to overcome language barriers. Congress authorized bilingual education in 1968 when it passed the Bilingual Education Act. This law was affirmed in the Supreme Court case of *Lau v. Nichols* (1974) [p. 192]. Bilingual education has always been controversial, and with the increased concern about immigration in the 1990s, it has become more controversial. In 1998, California voters passed a law that called for the end of bilingual education programs in the state [p. 194]. Be sure to review the CD-ROM module, ENGLISH ONLY, from Chapter 5.

Special Protection for Older Americans

Age discrimination is potentially the most widespread form of discrimination because it can effect everyone at some point in life. Congress passed the Age Discrimination Employment Act in 1967 [p. 195]. This law protects workers over the age of 40, and an amendment to the law, passed in 1978, prohibited mandatory retirement of most workers under the age of 70 [p. 196]. Older citizens tend to have the highest voter participation and have created a huge interest group, the American Association of Retired Persons (AARP), to protect their interests [p. 197].

Securing Rights for Persons with Disabilities

The Civil Rights Act of 1964 did not protect the rights of older Americans or the disabled. The landmark legislation to protect rights of persons with disabilities was the Americans with Disabilities Act of 1990. (ADA) This law requires employers to "reasonably accommodate" the needs of persons with disabilities. This has required physical access, which has led to increased facilities costs for government and business [p. 198]. These costs and the difficulty of interpreting the ADA have caused controversy. In 1998, the Supreme Court ruled that persons infected with HIV, the virus that causes AIDS, are under the protection of the ADA [p. 199].

The Rights and Status of Gay Males and Lesbians

The "Stonewall Riot" in 1969, in which gays and lesbians fought with police after a raid at a gay bar, created the movement for gay and lesbian rights. The movement has changed state laws on sexual relations between consenting adults and, in few states and over 150 cities, has achieved the passage of special laws against gay and lesbian discrimination. The trend toward more balanced state laws ended, however, in 1986 with the Supreme Court decision in *Bowers v. Hardwick*. This case upheld a Georgia law that made homosexual conduct between two adults a crime [p. 201].

The increased political activity of gays has not escaped the notice of politicians. Conservatives have generally been against gay rights, while liberals, like Jesse Jackson, have supported gay rights. In 1997, President Clinton became the first sitting president to address a gay rights organization. President Clinton was a leading force in developing a "Don't Ask, Don't Tell" policy to allow gays and lesbians to have careers in the military [p. 202]. Probably the most controversial aspect of gay rights is same-sex marriages and child custody issues. The Hawaii Supreme Court seems to have cleared the way for same-sex marriages in Hawaii. Other states have passed laws banning these marriages. In 1996, Congress passed the Defense of Marriage Act, which bans federal recognition of same-sex marriages [p. 203].

The Rights and Status of Juveniles

Children, defined as persons under the age sixteen, and in some cases under 18 or 21, have generally not had the same legal protections as adults—society assumes that parents protect their children. The Supreme Court began a slow evolution of children's rights with *Brown v. Board of Education of Topeka*, which was fully discussed in Chapter 5 [p. 204]. The *Brown* case granted children the status of rights-bearing persons. In *Yoder v. Wisconsin* (1972), the Court ruled that "children are 'persons' within the meaning of the Bill of Rights". The Twenty-sixth Amendment to the U.S. Constitution, ratified in 1971, granted the right to vote to citizens who are eighteen years old. The fact that eighteen-years-olds could be drafted, sent to fight, and possibly die in Vietnam, seemed to be a key factor in lowering the voting age [p. 205].

In civil and criminal cases, the age of majority, meaning the right to manage one's own affairs and have full enjoyment of civil rights, varies from eighteen to twenty-one years, depending on the state. In criminal cases, the concept of common law states that children from 7 to 14 years cannot commit a crime because they are not mature enough to understand what they are doing. Recent heinous crimes, such as the shooting deaths of four students and a teacher at a school in Jonesboro, Arkansas, by an 11- and 13-year-old, have caused some state officials to consider lowering the age at which a juvenile may be tried as an adult and faced with adult penalties, including the death penalty [p. 206-207].

Civil Rights—Beyond Equal Protection: Issues for the New Century

The growing proportion of those over sixty-five in the population will continue to challenge the funding and expenditures of public programs such as Social Security and Medicare. Persons with disabilities will continue to find new areas of employment and physical access that will challenge the definitions of the Americans with Disabilities Act. Clearly, discrimination continues against gay and lesbian persons and needs to be addressed. The debate of the rights of children will continue as the nation struggles with the problems of child abuse and violent crimes committed by children [p. 208].

KEY TERMS

affirmative action—p. 187

civil law—p. 205

common law—p. 206

criminal law—p. 205

majority—p. 206

mandatory retirement—p. 196

necessaries—p. 206

reverse discrimination—p. 188

C D- RO M *AMERICA AT ODDS*

AFFIRMITIVE ACTION. The interactive module for Chapter 6 deals with the issue of affirmative action. In 1965 President Johnson ordered the creation of affirmative action policies to remedy the effects of past discrimination. Students can view the key Supreme Court cases, such as *Bakke, Johnson,* and *Weber,* which helped define this issue. The module also looks at the recent Supreme Court decisions on affirmative action; Senators Jesse Helms of North Carolina, Carol Moseley-Braun of Illinois, and former Senator and Republican Presidential candidate Bob Dole give their viewpoints. A ten-question interactive quiz allows you to reinforce key points in the material.

PRACTICE EXAM

(Answers appear at the end of this chapter.)

Fill-in-the-Blank. Supply the missing word(s) or term(s) to complete the sentence.

1. The issue of _____ _____ was decided in the case of *Bakke v. University of California Regents.*

2. The *Hopwood* case brought an end to _____ _____ programs at the University of Texas.

3. The Civil Rights Act of 1991 added _____ to Title VII of the Civil Rights Act of 1964.

4. The right to a bilingual education was decided in the case of _____ v. _____ (1974).

5. Initially, the Age Discrimination in Employment Act did not address the issue of _____ _____.

6. The most significant federal legislation to affect the rights of persons with disabilities is the

_____ _____ _____ Act.

7. The Stonewall incident marked the beginning of the movement for _____.

8. The "don't ask, don't tell" policy is directed at _____ and _____ in the military.

9. There are no laws aimed specifically at protecting rights of children because our society presumes that

_____ protect their children.

10. Common law generally assumes that a child under _____ cannot understand the wrongful

nature of a crime that he or she has committed.

True/False. Circle the appropriate letter to indicate if the statement is true or false.

1. T F Affirmative Action is a policy to improve employment and educational opportunities for women and minorities.

2. T F The BAKKE case declared affirmative action unconstitutional in any form.

3. T F Proposition 209 in California ended all tax exemptions for citizens over 65 years old.

4. T F Some of the strongest critics of bilingual education are parents of Hispanic children who have been in these programs.

5. T F Mandatory retirement rules are now outlawed, except for a few select cases.

6. T F Individuals with AIDS are covered under the American with Disabilities Act of 1990.

7. T F Perhaps the most sensitive political issue affecting the rights of gay and lesbian couples is whether they should be allowed to marry.

8. T F The Supreme Court has ruled that children are "persons" under the meaning of the Bill of Rights.

9. T F Since the passage of the 26th Amendment, 18 to 20 year olds have had the highest voter turnout of any age group.

10. T   F   If an individual is legally a minor, he or she cannot be held responsible for most signed contracts.

Multiple-Choice. Circle the correct response.

1.   The policy steps taken to overcome the present effects of past discrimination is called

     a.   affirmative action.

     b.   legal justification.

     c.   equalizing lawsuit.

     d.   statutory worth.

2.   The ruling of the Supreme Court in the *Bakke* case

     a.   eliminated all affirmative action in higher education.

     b.   upheld all affirmative action in higher education.

     c.   eliminated racial quotas in affirmative action.

     d.   upheld the use of racial quotas in affirmative action.

3.   The case that directly challenged the *Bakke* decision was

     a.   *Hopwood v. State of Texas.*

     b.   *Lau v. Nichols.*

     c.   *Bowers v. Hardwick.*

     d.   *Wisconsin v. Yoder.*

4.   The concept of "English-immersion" is a direct challenge to

     a.   the rights of the disabled.

     b.   the rights of older Americans.

     c.   bilingual education.

     d.   the rights of juveniles.

5.   The problems of aging and retirement are going to become increasingly important national issues because

     a.   the President and Congress are getting older.

     b.   the population is steadily growing older.

     c.   nursing home owners are a powerful national lobby.

     d.   the elderly are taking jobs from younger workers.

6.   Mandatory retirement rules

     a.   were prohibited by the Civil Rights Act of 1964.

     b.   were prohibited by the Civil Rights Act of 1991.

     c.   were prohibited by an amendment to the Age Discrimination in Employment Act.

     d.   still apply to most professions, including teaching.

7. Voter participation, used as a measure of political involvement, illustrates that

    a. younger voters are very active.

    b. voting reaches a peak in middle-age and then declines.

    c. older voters participate in the highest percentages.

    d. there are more older people than the other age groups, so they have more voters.

8. The Americans with Disabilities Act requires

    a. the hiring of unqualified job applicants with disabilities.

    b. free public transportation for individuals with disabilities.

    c. "reasonable accommodation" to the needs of persons with disabilities.

    d. free medical insurance for individuals with disabilities.

9. The ruling in the case of *Bowers v. Hardwick* provided that

    a. same-sex individuals could legally marry

    b. anti-gay legislation is unconstitutional.

    c. homosexual conduct between adults is a crime.

    d. special laws protecting gay and lesbian rights are constitutional.

10. Same-sex marriages are

    a. legal in the state of Hawaii.

    b. prohibited in all states by the 1996 Defense of Marriage Act passed by Congress.

    c. not legal under the U.S. Constitution.

    d. legal under the "don't ask, don't tell" policy of President Clinton.

11. The first President to address a gay rights organization was

    a. President Truman.

    b. President Nixon.

    c. President Bush.

    d. President Clinton.

12. The reason the rights of children lack protection under the law is the presumption of our society and lawmakers that children

    a. need no protection.

    b. have all the laws necessary for their protection.

    c. do not need government interfering in their lives.

    d. are protected by their parents.

13. The age of majority for a person is

    a. 14 years old.

    b. 15 years old.

    c. 16 years old.

    d. variable from 18 to 21 depending on the state.

14. The aim of the juvenile court system is to

    a. punish the offending youth by incarceration.

    b. hold the youthful offender until he or she can be tried as an adult.

    c. teach good human contact.

    d. reform rather than to punish the youthful offender.

15. A juvenile's rights in a criminal case are

    a. the same as an adult.

    b. the same as their parents.

    c. limited, unless the judge determines they should be tried as adults.

    d. determined by their attorney.

Short Essay Questions. Briefly address the major concepts raised by the following questions.

1. Examine the concept of affirmative action and discuss the defining Supreme Court cases.

2. Explain the major issues that concern older Americans.

3. Describe the current rights of juveniles in both civil and criminal areas.

4. Explain the rights and status of gay and lesbian individuals in our society. Discuss the important cases or laws.

ANSWERS TO THE PRACTICE EXAM

Fill-in-the-Blank.

1. reverse discrimination [p. 188]   6. Americans with Disabilities [p. 198]

2. affirmative action [p. 189]   7. gay & lesbian rights [p. 201]

3. amendments [p. 189]   8. gays and lesbians [p. 202]

4. LAU V. NICHOLS [p. 192]   9. parents [p. 204]

5. mandatory retirement [p. 196]   10. fourteen years [p. 206]

True/False.

1. T [p. 187]	3. F [p. 190]	5. T [p. 196]	7. T [p. 203]	9. F [p. 205]
2. F [p. 188]	4. T [p. 194]	6. T [p. 198]	8. T [p. 205]	10. T [p. 206]

Multiple Choice.

1. a [p. 189]	4. c [p. 194]	7. c [p. 197]	10. a [p. 203]	13. d [p. 206]
2. c [p. 188]	5. b [p. 194]	8. c [p. 198]	11. d [p. 202]	14. d [p. 206]
3. a [p. 189]	6. c [p. 196]	9. c [p. 201]	12. d [p. 204]	15. a [p. 207]

Short Essay Answers

An adequate short answer consists of several paragraphs that relate to concepts addressed by the question. Always demonstrate your knowledge of the ideas by giving examples. The following represent major ideas that should be included in these short essays.

1. Examine the concept of affirmative action and discuss the defining Supreme Court cases [p. 187-191].

   - Affirmative action is special consideration or treatment to disadvantaged groups in an effort to overcome present effects of past discrimination.

   - *Bakke v. University of California regents* (1978) ruled on the concept of reverse discrimination against those who do not have minority status. The Court ruled that specific quotas are unconstitutional, but affirmative action was constitutional.

   - *Firefighters Local Union No. 1784 v. Stotts* (1984) ruled that affirmative action did not overturn seniority in determining layoffs.

   - *Hopwood v. State of Texas* (1996) ruled that race and other factors could not be used for determining admission to professional school. This case basically ruled existing affirmative action programs unconstitutional.

   - Proposition 209, passed in California in 1996, ended all state-sponsored affirmative action programs.

2. Explain the major issues that concern older Americans [p. 194-197].

   - Age discrimination is potentially the most widespread form of discrimination because anyone could be a victim at some point in his or her life.

   - Older Americans are very concerned about losing their jobs to younger, lower-salaried workers.

   - The Age Discrimination in Employment Act of 1967 (ADEA) gave protection to older workers. Originally the Act did not protect workers from mandatory retirement, but this was added by amendment in 1978.

   - Older Americans are very concerned about Social Security and medical benefits. They have formed a huge interest group (AARP) to maintain spending for these programs.

3. Explain the rights and status of gay and lesbian individuals in our society. Discuss the important cases or laws [p. 200-204].

   - The 1969 Stonewall riot at a New York City gay bar marked the beginning of the gay and lesbian rights movement.

   - During the 1970s and 1980s many state and local laws against gays and lesbian were repealed.

   - In *Bowers v. Hardwick* (1986), however, the Supreme Court ruled that state laws prohibiting homosexual contact between adults were constitutional. In *Romer v. Evans* (1996), the Court ruled that states could not pass laws that take all legal protections from homosexuals.

- President Clinton established a "don't ask, don't tell" policy to allow gays and lesbians to have careers in the military. This policy has been controversial and has critics on both sides of the debate.
- In 1996, the Hawaii Supreme Court cleared the way for same-sex marriages in that state. This controversy has been even greater than the issue of homosexuals serving in military. Congress, in the Defense of Marriage Act, and at least 16 states and have passed laws banning same-sex marriages.
- Child-custody rights are also difficult for gay and lesbian parents.

4. Describe the current rights of juveniles in both civil and criminal areas [p. 204-207].
   - Juveniles do not have the legal rights of adults because it is assumed that parents will protect their children.
   - The Supreme Court in *Yoder v. Wisconsin* (1972) ruled that children are "persons" under the meaning of the Bill of Rights.
   - The rights of juveniles depend upon the age of majority. This concept means the age at which a person is entitled by law to manage his or her own affairs and have full civil rights. This varies from 18 to 21 years old depending upon the state.
   - In Civil cases, juveniles cannot be held responsible for contracts, unless it is for necessaries (things necessary for subsistence as determined by the court).
   - In Criminal cases, juveniles do not have the same due process rights as adults, but usually do not face the same penalties. In common law, it is presumed that children under fourteen do not understand the nature of their crimes. Recent mass murders by children under fourteen at a school in Jonesboro, Arkansas, have challenged the concept of when a child may be tried as an adult and receive adult punishment, even the death penalty.

Chapter 7
Public Opinion

CHAPTER SUMMARY

How Powerful is Public Opinion?

Public opinion against the war in Vietnam seemed to be a factor in 1968, when President Lyndon Johnson declined to run for re-election. Public opinion on the scandal surrounding the 1972 Watergate break-in gave Congress strong support to initiate impeachment proceeding against President Nixon. It appears that public support for President Clinton in the Monica Lewinsky scandal may influence Congress in current impeachment proceedings [p. 217-218].

Defining Public Opinion

Public opinion is defined as the aggregate of individual attitudes or beliefs shared by some portion of adults. Public opinion is made known in a democracy by protests, demonstrations, and lobbying by interest groups. In the age of the Internet, citizens use their personal computers to send opinions to government officials [p. 218]. There are very few issues on which most Americans agree. When a large proportion of the public does appear to hold the same view on an issue, a consensus exists. If opinion is polarized between two quite different positions, divisive opinion exists. See Figure 7-1 and 7-2, p. 219, for examples of each of these concepts. Public opinion has five major qualities:

- intensity—the strength of a position for or against a public policy
- fluidity—the extent to which public opinion changes over time
- stability—the extent to which opinion remains constant over a period of time
- relevance—the extent to which an issue is a concern at a particular time
- the level of political knowledge—a factor that influences the four other qualities [p. 220-222].

Measuring Public Opinion: Polling Techniques

In the 1800s, newspapers and magazines used face-to-face straw polls to attract readers. In the 20th century, the magazine *Literary Digest* developed modern techniques by mailing questionnaires to subscribers. In 1936, the magazine's poll predicted that Alfred Landon would defeat Franklin Roosevelt for President. Landon won only two states. The most important principle in poll taking is randomness [p. 223]. If drawn from a truly random sample of opinions, a poll should be relatively accurate. Gallup and Roper polls interview about 1,500 individuals to get within a margin of error of 3%. [p. 224]. See Table 7-1 for the margins of error since 1936. Public opinion polls are snapshots of opinions at a specific time on a specific question. The timing of the poll, a sampling error of interviewing too few people, and the wording of the question, can all create an inaccurate prediction of a political outcome.

Chapter 7   Public Opinion

How Opinion is Formed.

The process by which individuals acquire political beliefs and opinion is called political socialization [p. 230]. The most important influence in this process is the family. Children have a strong need for parental approval, and are very receptive to the parent's opinions. The clearest family influence is the political party identification. Schools are also an important influence. Education seems to influence the level of activity in the political process. The more education a person receives the higher the level of political activity. Friendships and associations in peer groups can influence political attitudes [p. 231]. Religious associations also create political attitudes, although this is hard to measure. In recent years, over 42% of evangelical Protestants are Republicans. Wealth and social status influence political attitudes, although there is probably a strong correlation with the education factor in shaping wealth and social status. When events produce a long-term political impact, you have generational effects, which can influence political opinions. For example, voters who grew up in the 1930s during the Great Depression were likely to become Democrats [p. 232]. Some individuals have the ability to influence the opinions of others because of position, expertise or personality. Often these individuals, called opinion leaders, use the media to influence opinions. Finally, the election of Ronald Reagan in 1980 seemed to produce a gender gap, in which women were 5 or 6% more likely to vote for Democrats for President. This gap continued throughout the 1990s [p. 234].

Political Culture and Public Opinion

Although Americans are divided into numerous ethnic, religious, political groups, the American political culture binds us together with the core values of (1) liberty, equality, and property; (2) support for religion; and (3) community service and personal achievement. Another important element is the trust that individuals express in the government and political institutions. Unfortunately, trust in political institutions reached an all time low in 1992. See Table 7-2 on page 236.

Public Opinion about Government

Public opinion about the confidence in various institutions in our society has declined in the 1990s. Church and bank are lower than previous decades. The military and Supreme Court are government institutions that have the highest levels of confidence. See Table 7-3 on page 236. While the public may have little confidence in some government institutions, they still turn to government to solve major problems. See Table 7-4 page 238.

The Spectrum of Political Beliefs

Political candidates in American, frequently, identify themselves as liberal or conservative. Liberals are generally thought to support the national government intervening in the economy to ensure growth, to support social-welfare programs, and to be tolerant of social change. P. 238. Conservatives feel that national government has grown too big, that social-welfare should be greatly limited, and traditional family values should be supported. The largest number of individuals in society refers to themselves as moderate. Individuals who have a comprehensive world-view within a liberal or conservative ideology are called ideologues. Senator Edward Kennedy is an example of a liberal ideologue, while independent presidential candidates, Pat Buchanan is a conservative ideologue.

Public Opinion and the Political Process

While the exact influence of public opinion on government policy cannot be measured, it appears that politicians, who ignore public opinion, run a great risk of defeat in the next election.

Public Opinion: Issues for the New Century

Public opinion is a vital part of the political process. The over use of polls and poll results in the media seems to have caused a public reaction against this process. The sample of individuals willing to provide poll data is declining. This could be a dangerous trend, which makes it more difficult to accurately judge opinions on the serious issues effecting our society.

KEY TERMS

consensus—p. 219

divisive opinion—p. 219

fluidity—p. 221

gender gap—p. 234

generational effect —p. 232

ideologue—p. 240

intensity—p. 220

media—p. 233

opinion leader—p. 233

opinion poll—p. 222

peer group—p. 231

political socialization—p. 230

political trust—p. 235

public opinion—p. 218

sampling error—p. 227

stability—p. 221

PRACTICE EXAM

[Answers appear at the end of this chapter.]

Fill-in-the-Blank. Supply the missing word(s) or term(s) to complete the sentence.

1. The aggregate of individual attitudes and beliefs is _____ _____.

2. How much people will express their opinions determines the _____ of public opinion.

3. _____ _____ is polarized between two quite different positions.

4. For most people, _____ public opinion is public opinion on issues concerning them.

5. When a large proportion of the American public expresses the same view on an issue, we say that a

    _____ exists.

6. Roper. Gallup, and Crossley developed modern polling techniques to predict the total voting

    population by using _____ _____ with small samples of selected voters.

7. The most important principle in sampling public opinion is _____.

8. The _____ is the most important influence in political socialization.

9. _____ _____ is the term that describes the differences in issue

    orientation and voting behavior between men and women.

10. More individuals are likely to consider themselves_____ than as liberal or conservative.

True/False. Circle the appropriate letter to indicate if the statement is true or false.

1. T   F   Adverse public opinion in 1968 caused President Johnson to decline to run for re-election.
2. T   F   The level of political information possessed by the average person is very high.
3. T   F   Quota sampling is a more accurate technique for public opinion than random sampling.
4. T   F   Most studies show that children are socialized to accept their parents' political party.
5. T   F   Education has little to do with interest or activity in politics.

6. T   F   During the 1960s and 1970s, political trust declined steeply.

7. T   F   Generational effects can result in long-lasting attachments to political parties.

8. T   F   The government institution that the public has the most confidence in, is the military.

9. T   F   Election research suggests that a large percentage of Americans can be identified as political ideologues.

10. T   F   Well-defined public opinion tends to restrain government officials from taking unpopular actions.

Multiple-Choice. Circle the correct response.

1. The aggregate of individual attitudes or beliefs shared by some portion of adults is referred to as
    a. political opinion.
    b. Propaganda.
    c. public opinion.
    d. an ideology.

2. Intensity, fluidity, stability, latency and relevance are all qualities of
    a. propaganda.
    b. public opinion.
    c. editorial writing at major newspapers.
    d. political rhetoric

3. When public opinion is capable of changing drastically it is said to be
    a. stable
    b. relevant
    c. latent
    d. fluid

4. Until the post-World War II period, southern states consistently elected Democratic, rather than Republican, candidates to public office. This is an example of _____ of public opinion.
    a. fluidity
    b. relevancy
    c. stability
    d. intensity

5. The most important principle in sampling is
    a. a large sample
    b. picking an issue where consensus can be found
    c. randomness
    d. asking the right questions

6.   The influence of the family in political socialization is most likely to effect

a.   political participation

b.   political party choice

c.   lobbying to influence public policy

d.   authority figure choice

7.   Support for civil liberties and tolerance of different points of view is highest among

a.   people influenced by peer groups

b.   people influenced by religious associations

c.   people of lower economic status

d.   people of higher economic status

8.   The quality of public opinion, which is most like generational effects is

a.   fluidity

b.   stability

c.   intensity

d.   relevance

9.   Most views that are expressed as political opinions are acquired through a process known as

a.   political socialization

b.   propaganda

c.   enculturation

d.   education

10. A person's place of residence seems to effect political attitudes, with big city dwellers tending to be

a.   liberal and Democratic

b.   liberal and Republican

c.   conservative and Democratic

d.   conservative and Republican

11. The most important values in the American political system include

a.   federalism, unity, and freedom

b.   support for the president, Congress, and the courts

c.   liberty, equality, and property

d.   the two-party system, and respect for the Constitution

12. In the United States, the terms liberal and conservative refer to political positions that date from the

a.   Revolutionary War

b.   Great Depression

c.   Vietnam era

d.   Civil rights movement of the 1960s

13. Individuals who hold carefully thought out, consistent political beliefs are described as

    a.   ideologues

    b.   partisans

    c.   conservatives

    d.   liberals

14. A general description of American political ideology is that

    a.   about 50% of Americans are liberal and 50% conservative

    b.   most people have mixed sets of opinions that do not fit into one ideology

    c.   most Americans are liberal

    d.   ideology has no role in American politics

15. The impact of strong public opinion on government action

    a.   encourages officials to ignore public opinion

    b.   allows government officials to shape policy according to opinion polls

    c.   restrains officials from taking truly unpopular actions

    d.   discourages public officials from standing up for what is right.

Short Essay Questions. Briefly address the major concepts raised by the following questions.

1. Define the qualities of public opinion.

2. Describe the key factors in conducting opinion polls.

3. Explain the most important influences in political socialization.

4. Discuss the most important values of the American political system and the trends of political trust in the last three decades.

ANSWERS TO THE PRACTICE EXAM

Fill-in-the-Blank.

1. public opinion [p. 218]

2. intensity [p. 220]

3. divisive opinion [p. 219]

4. relevant [p. 221]

5. consensus [p. 219]

6. personal interviews [p. 223]

7. randomness [p. 223]

8. family [p. 230]

9. gender gap [p. 234]

10. moderate [p. 239]

True/False

1. T [p. 217]   3. F [p. 224]   5. F [p. 231]   7. T [p. 232]   9. F [p. 240]

2. F [p. 222]   4. T [p. 231]   6. T [p. 235]   8. T [p. 236]   10. T [p. 240]

Multiple Choice.

1. c [p. 218]	4. c [p. 221]	7. d [p. 232]	10. a [p. 234]	13. a [p. 240]
2. b [p. 220]	5. c [p. 227]	8. b [p. 232]	11. c [p. 235]	14. b [p. 240]
3. d [p. 221]	6. b [p. 230]	9. a [p. 230]	12. b [p. 238]	15. c [p. 240]

Short Essay Answers.

An adequate short answer consists of several paragraphs that discuss the concepts addressed by the question. Always demonstrate your knowledge of the ideas by giving examples. The following represent major ideas that should be included in these short essays.

1. Define the qualities of public opinion [p. 220-222].

    Public opinion has five identifiable qualities.

    *   Intensity is how strongly people are willing to express their private opinions. Immigration to the United States has been an intensely felt issue the last few years.

    *   Fluidity is the drastic change in public opinion in a relatively short period of time. The collapse of the Cold War, and Russia's emergence as a democracy has led to a radical change of opinion about whether Russia is our enemy.

    *   Stability is individual opinion that remains constant over a lifetime. Taken together, these opinions can have a major impact on public opinion. The Solid South concept of democratic candidates usually winning elections in southern states is a good example of stability.

    *   Relevance is the extent to which an issue is of concern at a particular time. For example, when individuals age, they become much more concerned about the safety of the Social Security program, and are much more likely to express opinions about that program.

    *   Political knowledge is tied to relevance and intensity. The more strongly interested in an issue, the more likely a person is to find out more about the issue. If people are not interested in an issue, they probably won't know much about it.

2. Describe the key factors in conducting opinion polls [p. 222-229].

    There are three key factors in conducting accurate public opinion polls.

    *   Randomness is the most important factor. The sample to be interviewed must be representative of the whole population. One technique is to choose a random sample of telephone numbers. A quota sampling, which is not as accurate, is to select people who represent certain types of people. The major polls can interview about 1,500 people and predict elections within a margin of three percent, plus or minus.

    *   Timing is a second factor. Polls continue to be conducted until the election day because a shift in opinion at the last minute can produce an unexpected outcome. The polls in the presidential

election of 1980 between Carter and Reagan showed a very close contest. Reagan won easily, because of a shift in the undecided vote in the last week of the election.

- The types of questions asked on the survey have a major impact on the results of the poll. If poorly worded or leading questions are asked, the result will be distorted.

3. Explain the most important influences in political socialization [p. 230-234].

   Political socialization is the process by which individuals acquire political beliefs and attitudes.

   - The family is the most important influence and largely responsible for political party choice.
   - Schools are most likely to influence the understanding of issues and political activity.
   - Peer groups most strongly influence direct involvement in political activity.
   - Religion has some impact on political activity, but its influence is not clear.
   - Wealth and social-class influence a tolerance for differences and more voting activity.
   - Generational events, such as the great Depression, can influence opinion for decades.
   - Charismatic opinion leaders using the power of media can have a tremendous impact on opinion.
   - The demographic factors of age, gender, location, and region of residence have the final influences on the process we call political socialization.

4. Discuss the most important values of the American political system and the trend in political trust over the last three decades [p. 235-238].

   The core elements of the American political system include:

   - Liberty, equality, and property.
   - Support for religion.
   - Community service and personal achievement.

   These generally-supported values provide an environment of support for the political system, which helps the system survive a crisis such as scandal. The levels of political trust that citizens have in the system declined tremendously in the 1960s and 1970s and reached an all-time low in 1992. The military and the Supreme Court are the most trusted parts of the political system today. It remains to be seen, if the current Clinton scandal will set new all-time lows in political trust.

Chapter 8
Interest Groups

CHAPTER SUMMARY

The attempt by the tobacco industry to come to an agreement with national and state governments to avoid lawsuits and very strict regulation is an excellent example of an interest group lobbying to preserve its economic interest [p. 247].

The Role of Interest Groups

Pluralist theory, discussed in Chapter 1, says that the structure of American government invites a political process of competition amoung interest groups. Famed French visitor, Alexis de Tocqueville observed in 1834, that American seemed to be a nation of joiners of associations [p. 248].

The Benefits of Interest Groups

According to the theory of Mancur Olson, it is not rational for individuals to join groups. If a group is successful in getting some benefit, how can that benefit be denied to others in the same situation. Why pay union dues, if workers benefits achieved by the union go to all workers? It is more logical to wait for others to gain benefits and then share them. People need incentives to join groups. The three major incentives are

- solidary, which include companionship, a sense of belonging, and the pleasure of associations
- material, which are economic benefits or opportunities
- purposive, which relate to one's ethical beliefs or ideological principles[p. 250].

Interest Groups and Social Movements

Interest groups often arise from mass social movements, which represent the demands for major social change of a large segment of the population. The Civil Rights movement of the 1950s and 1960s is a good example of a social movement [p. 251].

Types of Interest Groups

Although thousands of groups exist, they can be discussed in a few broad categories.

- Economic interest groups include business, agriculture, labor, public employee, and professional organizations.
    - ◊ The largest business groups are the National Association of Manufactures (NAM), U.S. Chamber of Commerce, and the Business Roundtable.
    - ◊ American farmers have been very successful lobbying for government support, despite representing only about 2 percent of U.S. workers. The American Farm Bureau and the National Farmers' Union are the most powerful agriculture groups [p. 252].
- Labor unions have tired to balance the power of business groups, but have weakened in recent years. The biggest union is the giant AFL-CIO. Public employee interest groups have grown in recent years. These groups are similar to unions, but lack the legal power to strike, which has not stopped them from strikes. One of the biggest of these unions is the American Federation of State,

County, Municipal Employees (AFSCME) [p. 254].

3.   Professional occupations, such as lawyers, and doctors are well represented in the American Bar Association and American Medical Association [p. 256].

4.   Environmental interest groups actually began in the early part of the century with the National Audubon Society and the Sierra Club. Mass memberships groups have been created since Earth Day in 1972; they include the National Wildlife Federation and the Nature Conservancy.

5.   Public interest groups, concerned with the public good, have been created almost single-handedly by consumer activist, Ralph Nader. Some of the largest public interest groups that have developed without Nader's help are Common Cause and the American Civil Liberties Union [p. 257].

6.   Special interest groups, sometimes called single-interest groups, can be very effective concentrating resources on a single issue. The National Rifle Association, and the American Association of Retired Persons are good examples of a special interest group [p.258].

7.   Finally, foreign governments of the largest trading partners of the U.S. hire lobbyists to try to influence trade policy. Japan, South Korea, Canada, and the European Union (EU) are just a few of the foreign government interest groups [p 259]. See Table 8-1 page 253 for a more detailed list of the different types of interest groups.

Interest Group Strategies

Interest group influence can be divided into direct techniques and indirect techniques. The direct techniques use lobbying, public ratings of government officials, and campaign contributions [p. 259]. Lobbyists are private citizens who meet public officials on behalf of the interests they represent. See page 260 for a list of lobbying activities. Many groups will publish the voting records of legislators on issues of interest to the group. Political Action Committees (PACs) represent the latest technique to directly influence politics. These PACs, which have grown to over 4,500 in the 1990s, are a major source of campaign contributions to candidates. In the 1994 election for the House of Representatives, 32 percent of all campaign contributions came from PACs [p. 262].

Indirect techniques use the general public or individuals to influence the government for the interest group. Interest groups will try to generate a "groundswell" of support through mass mailing and advertising, or use constituents to lobby the lawmaker. The "shotgun" approach tries to get as many people as possible to write or call or E-mail. In the "rifle" approach, the group tries to get a few influential constituents to talk to the lawmaker. Climate control describes a public relation technique that tries to create favorable public opinion about a group or industry [p. 263]. Lastly, a group may form an alliance with other groups that are concerned with the same legislation [p. 264].

Regulating Lobbyists

The first attempt to regulate lobbyists and lobbying activities was the Legislative Reorganization Act of 1946. This law was ruled constitutional in the Supreme Court case of *United States v. Harriss* in

1954. The Court upheld a narrow interpretation of the law, which meant that very few lobbyists actually registered under the law. In 1995, Congress passed a far-reaching lobby regulation law that should require 3 to 10 times as many lobbyists to register. Congress also decided to change the rules covering gifts and travel expenses. See page 266 for a list of the major provisions of the law.

Interest Groups and Representative Democracy

The role of interest groups in our democracy is a continuing topic of debate. Members of interest groups are middle or upper-class in background; leaders of interest groups, because they are often from a higher social class than the membership, can be called an "elite within an elite." Pluralist theory presumes that groups compete with each other for the benefit of the members, but the strong presence of elites across categories complicates the activity. In the overall analysis, it is clear that even the most powerful interest group does not always prevail. By definition, an interest group can only be effective on the narrow range of interests that hold the group together. When an interest group tries address broad policy issues, it fragments its membership base and cannot influence policy.

Interest Groups: Issues for the New Century

The role of interest groups in American society has been debated since the writing of the Constitution. In the *Federalist Papers,* James Madison warned against the "spirit of faction." Future debate is focused on the issue of campaign contributions by interest groups. One possible solution is public financing, which is used in the presidential election. Groups will continue to prosper in the future because they provide real opportunities for more and more citizens to participate in and influence the political process.

KEY TERMS

climate control—p. 263

direct technique—p. 259

indirect technique—p. 259

interest group—p. 247

lobbying—p. 247

material incentive—p. 250

political action committee (PAC)—p. 261

public interest—p. 257

purposive incentive—p. 251

service sector—p. 254

social movement—p. 251

solidary incentive—p. 250

CD-ROM *AMERICA AT ODDS*

GUN CONTROL. The interactive module for Chapter 8 discusses the issue of gun control legislation and the meaning of the Second Amendment in the Bill of Rights. The U.S. Supreme Court in the case of Lewis v. U.S. (1980) ruled that the Second Amendment does not provide for individual gun ownership, unless it is related to militia duty. Interactive questions encourage the reader to explore the Assault Weapons Ban and the Brady Bill. Hear two members of Congress, Patrick Kennedy of Rhode Island, and Gerald Solomon of New York debate the Gun Control issue. A ten-question interactive multiple-choice quiz reinforces key points in the material.

PRACTICE EXAM

[Answers appear at the end of this chapter.]

Fill-in-the-Blank. Supply the missing word(s) or term(s) to complete the sentence.

1. An interest group must give individuals an _____ to become members.

2. _____ _____ represent the demands of a large segment of the public for social change.

3. Numerous interest groups in the United States have been formed to promote _____ interests.

4. Despite representing only about 2% of the population, _____ interest groups have

   been very successful in receiving government aid.

5. Since 1965, the degree of unionization in the _____ sector has declined, but has grown

   among _____ employees.

6. The most well-known public interest groups have been organized by consumer activist, _____.

7. The nation's largest interest group is the _____ _____ _____ _____.

8. Interest groups use techniques that may be divided into _____ and _____.

9. Over the last two decades, the most important form of campaign help from interest groups has come

   from their _____ _____ _____.

10. _____ _____ describes a public relations strategy to improve a group's image.

True/False. Circle the appropriate letter to indicate if the statement is true or false.

1. T F The structure of our political system makes it difficult for individuals and groups to exert influence on the system.
2. T F James Madison was a firm believer in strengthening interest group activity.
3. T F The strength of union membership has traditionally been in the service workforce.
4. T F Foreign governments are prohibited from lobbying in the United States.
5. T F The use of public relations techniques to influence public opinion about a group is called the rifle approach.
6. T F In the last twenty years, the influence of political action committees in the campaign process has diminished.
7. T F Using constituents to lobby for a group's goals is a most effective interest group technique.
8. T F Most interest groups have a middle-class or upper-class bias.
9. T F The Federal Regulation of Lobbying Act regulates all forms of lobbying at the national level.
10. T F Interest groups allow individuals to influence government far beyond just voting.

Multiple-Choice. Circle the correct response.

1. Any organized group whose members share common objectives and actively attempt to influence the government is a(n)
    a. political party.
    b. bureaucracy.
    c. interest group.
    d. institution.

2. Individuals and groups can exert influence at many different points in our government because
    a. officials are always looking for campaign contributions.
    b. interest group members are also voters.
    c. of the structure of our political system.
    d. we have a unitary form of government.

3. A sense of belonging and the pleasure of associating with others provide _____ to join an interest group.
    a. material incentives
    b. purposive incentives
    c. solidary incentives
    d. herd incentives

4. Interest groups are often spawned by mass

    a. increases of young voters.

    b. publication of "underground" newspapers.

    c. factionalism.

    d. social movements.

5. The role of labor unions in American society has weakened in recent years, as witnessed by

    a. the rise of business groups.

    b. a decline in union membership.

    c. the lack of effective leadership.

    d. an increase in government regulation.

6. Since 1965, the greatest growth in unionization has occurred in the unionization of

    a. military personnel.

    b. professional athletes.

    c. public employees.

    d. private sector employees.

7. Lobbying, rating legislative behavior, and campaign assistance are

    a. the main indirect techniques used by interest groups.

    b. considered ineffective methods of swaying votes.

    c. the main direct techniques used by interest groups.

    d. considered obsolete in view of today's modern technology.

8. The bulk of campaign contributions from interest groups goes to

    a. presidential candidates.

    b. liberals more than conservatives.

    c. candidates who face little or no opposition.

    d. challengers rather than incumbents.

9. The *U.S. v Harriss* case ruled that the Federal Regulation of Lobbying Act

    a. is constitutional.

    b. is unconstitutional.

    c. should be left to the states to regulate.

    d. only applies to presidential elections.

10. The "shotgun" approach to lobbying consists of

    a. mobilizing large numbers of constituents to write or phone their legislators.

    b. identifying specific constituents to write or phone their legislators.

    c. concentrating only on gun control issues.

    d. allowing lobbyists to determine the most appropriate strategy.

11.   One of the benefits of forming alliances between interest groups is that

    a.   it is easier to keep track of interest groups if they are fewer in numbers.

    b.   it makes it easier to solicit contributions.

    c.   there is strength in numbers.

    d.   it shares expenses and multiplies the influence.

12.   The recent changes of the Federal Regulation of Lobbying Act are expected to

    a.   decrease the number of registered lobbyists.

    b.   increase the number of registered lobbyists three to ten times what it is currently.

    c.   eliminate registering lobbyists.

    d.   provide lobbyists with less money to use to influence the government.

13.   Interest groups tend to have a

    a.   lower-class bias.

    b.   middle to upper-class bias.

    c.   neutral bias.

    d.   democratic foundation for decision-making.

14.   The nation's largest interest group is (the)

    a.   American Association of Retired Persons.

    b.   Common Cause.

    c.   National Education Association.

    d.   National Rifle Association.

15.   The great advantage for democracy in interest group activity is that

    a.   it is a way to demonstrate support for governmental policy.

    b.   individual citizens are empowered to influence government.

    c.   it serves as a basis of political party organization.

    d.   it is a way to monitor the activities of Congress.

Short Essay Questions. Briefly address the major concepts raised by the following questions.

1.   Discuss the incentives for an individual to join an interest group.

2.   Describe the various types of major interest groups.

3.   Explain the direct techniques used by interest groups to influence government.

4.   Discuss the indirect techniques used by interest groups to influence government.

ANSWERS TO THE PRACTICE EXAM

Fill-in-the-Blank.

1. incentive [p. 250]
2. Social movements [p. 251]
3. economic [p. 252]
4. agricultural [p. 252]
5. private, public [p. 254]
6. Ralph Nader [p. 257]
7. American Association of Retired Persons [p. 258]
8. direct, indirect [p. 259]
9. Political Action Committees (PAC) [p. 261
10. Climate control [p. 263]

True/False

1. F [p. 248]
2. F [p. 248]
3. F [p. 254]
4. F [p. 259]
5. F [p. 263]
6. F [p. 261]
7. T [p. 263]
8. T [p. 266]
9. F [p. 265]
10. T [p. 268]

Multiple-Choice.

1. c [p. 247]
2. c [p. 248]
3. c [p. 250]
4. d [p. 251]
5. b [p. 254]
6. c [p. 254]
7. c [p. 259]
8. c [p. 262]
9. a [p. 265]
10. a [p. 263]
11. d [p. 264]
12. b [p. 266]
13. b [p. 266]
14. a [p. 267]
15. b [p. 268]

Short Essays.

An adequate short answer consists of several paragraphs that address concepts raised by the question. Always demonstrate your knowledge of the ideas by giving examples. The following represent major ideas that should be included in these short essays.

1. Discuss the incentives for an individual to join an interest group [p. 250-251].

   * There are three major incentives for individuals to join interest groups, solidary, material, and purposive.
   * Solidary incentives include companionship, a sense of belonging, and the pleasure of associating with others
   * Material incentives are economic benefits or opportunities, such as discounts, insurance, or travel planning.
   * Purposive incentives provide the satisfaction of taking action for one's beliefs or principles.

2. Describe the various types of interest groups [p. 252-259].

   * The major types of interest groups are economic, environmental, public, special, and foreign governments.
   * Economic interest groups include business, agricultual, labor, public employees, and professional.

- Environmental interest groups began in 1905 with the National Audubon society. More recent groups include the National Wildlife Federation, and the Nature Conservancy.

- Public interest groups were greatly influenced by consumer activist Ralph Nader. One of the largest public interest groups today is Common Cause.

- Special interest, or single-interest, groups focus on one issue such as abortion or gun control.

- Foreign governments that are major trading partners of the U.S. lobby for trade concessions and aid from the U.S. government.

3. Explain the direct techniques used by interest groups to influence government [p. 259-262].

   - There are three important direct techniques of interest group influence. These are lobbying, rating legislators, and campaign assistance.

   - Lobbying entails a range of activities that include private meetings, testifying in public meetings, drafting legislation, providing political information, and social occasions.

   - Rating legislators by their votes on issues important to the group provides the members of the group with important information on which candidates to support.

   - Campaign assistance in the form of campaign contributions has grown tremendously in the past two decades because of the increase in the number of Political Action Committees (PAC). PACs account for about one-third of all campaign contributions.

4. Discuss the indirect techniques used by interest groups to influence government [p. 262-264].

   - Indirect techniques allow interest groups to influence government policy by using the general public, individual constituents, and other interest groups.

   - Interest groups try to create a "groundswell" of public opinion by using mass advertising. Sometimes, public relations techniques are used to create favorable public opinion toward the interest. This technique is known as climate control.

   - The use of individual constituents is one of the most successful techniques. The attempt to mobilize as many constituents as possible is know as the "shotgun" approach. An attempt to mobilize very influential constituents is called the "rifle" approach.

   - Building an alliance with other interest groups on common issues allows groups to share costs and multiply their influence.

Chapter 9
Political Parties

CHAPTER SUMMARY

What is a Political Party?

A political party is a group of political activists who organize to win elections, to operate the government, and to determine public policy. A faction is a group within the party that acts together to pursue a particular point of view [p. 275].

Function of Political Parties in the United States

Political parties have five basic functions. These are:

- recruiting candidates for public office
- organizing and running elections
- presenting alternative policies
- accepting responsibility for operating the government
- acting as the organized opposition to the party in power [p. 275-276].

A Short History of Political Parties in the United States

See Figure 9-1 page 277 for a look at the different political parties in the U.S. from 1789. The evolution of our political party system can be divided into six periods.

- The first period from 1789 to 1812 saw the creation of political parties. The Federalists favored adoption of the Constitution and the Anti-Federalists opposed adoption.
- The second period from 1816 to 1824, when elections centered on individual candidates rather than parties, was the era of personal politics [p. 278].
- The third period, from Andrew Jackson's presidency to the Civil War, 1828-1860, saw the birth and death of the Whig party.
- The fourth period from 1864 to 1892 encompassed the creation of the heavily Democratic South and the heavily Republican North.
- The next period from 1896 to 1928 saw the development of the Progressive Party, which ran Theodore Roosevelt for President in 1912 [p. 279].
- The final period is the modern era from 1932 to the present. President Franklin Roosevelt's New Deal created the political landscape that we have today [p. 280].

The Three Faces of a Party

Each political party consists of three major components. These are

- the party-in-the-electorate, people who express a preference for one party over the other
- the party organization, which covers the structure, staff, and official members of the party
- the party-in-government, the elected and appointed government officials [p. 281].

Party Organization

American political parties have a standard, pyramid-shaped organization. See Figure 9-2 page 282. At each national convention, the national party organization selects the national committee and national chairperson to direct the party during the four-year period between conventions [p. 284].The state party organization consists of a state committee, state chairperson, and a number of local organizations. States parties are important in national politics because of the unit rule, which allots electoral votes in an indivisible bloc (except in Maine and Nebraska). The lowest level of party organization, called the grass roots, is composed of county and district party officials, precinct chairpersons, and party workers. The political machine no longer exists because of the decline of patronage. Local political organization can still have a major impact on elections, particularly local elections [p. 285-287].

The Party and its Members

The core of the Democratic Party is minorities, the working class, and various ethnic groups. Democrats generally support government intervention in the economy to help individuals in need. The Republican Party draws its support from college graduates, upper-income families, and professionals or businesspersons. Republicans support the private marketplace, and believe that the government should be involved in fewer social programs [p. 288]. See Figure 9-3 page 289 for a survey on which party is better at various policy areas.

The Party-in-Government

When the party elects its members to hold government office, various factors limit the ability of the party to carry out its programs. The American system of checks-and-balances restrains a given party because the voters seems to prefer a "divided government"—with the executive and legislative branches controlled by different parties. This is evident in the increasing trend of ticket splitting. There is also a lack of cohesion in American parties, which means that parties cannot count on every elected member to support the programs of the party [p. 189].

Why Do We Have a Two-Party System?

The historical development of the Federalists and Anti-Federalists laid the foundation for two political parties holding two distinct sets of interests [p. 291]. The political socialization of children toward identification with the party of the parent has been an important factor in maintaining the already-established two-party system [p. 292]. The political culture has been one of consensus and moderation. This has helped to maintain the two-party system. The winner-take-all election system, particularly in the Electoral College, makes it very difficult for third parties to have any electoral success [p. 293]. Finally, most state and federal election laws provide a clear advantage to the two major parties. Third party candidates for President are not eligible for federal matching funds [p. 294]. See "Getting on the Ballot" for state election laws on page 295.

The Role of Minor Parties in U.S. Political History

Minor parties have not been able to compete successfully against the two major parties, but have played an important role in our political life. The most successful minor parties split from the major parties. In 1912, the Bull Moose Progressive Party, splitting from the Republican pary, nominated Theodore Roosevelt for President, created a three-way race, and gave the election to Democrat Woodrow Wilson [p. 296]. The American Independent Party, a Democratic splinter party, supported George Wallace for President in 1968; although he received 46 electoral votes, this did not significantly affect Richard Nixon's victory. The third party candidate in 1992, H. Ross Perot, probably took votes away from Republican George Bush to give the victory to Democrat Bill Clinton [p. 298].

Ideologically-based parties, such as the Socialist Party, remain active today, and had real electoral success in the early twentieth century. Other minor parties, for example, the Greenback and Populist parties, have organized around specific economic issues and then disappeared [p. 297]. Minor parties have influenced American politics by raising important political issues that are usually adopted by one of the major parties, and, in some cases, determine the outcome of the presidential election. The current state of political party identification indicates a movement away from the two major parties. Thirty-four percent of voters today classify themselves as independents. See Figure 9-4 page 299.

Political Parties: Issues for the New Century

American political parties face a number of challenges for the future. Parties must address what they offer voters, what to do about independent candidates that can fund their own campaigns or form their own political parties, and whether the major parties stand for different positions on the issues [p. 301].

KEY TERMS

cadre—p. 276

divided government—p. 280

Electoral College—p. 293

Era of Personal Politics—p. 278

CD-ROM *AMERICA AT ODDS*

THE CHANGING FACE OF POLITICAL PARTIES.   The interactive module for Chapter 9 discusses the platforms and issues of the two major political parties. Look at the history of the party platforms in interactive questions. The major political parties do take significant action to attempt to carry out about 75% of their platform. In spite of the public myth about what the parties stand for, there are significant differences between the parties on some issues. An interactive exercise encourages the reader to build the two major party platforms for the 1996 presidential election. A ten-question interactive multiple-choice quiz reinforces key points in the material.

PRACTICE EXAM

[Answers appear at the end of this chapter.]

Fill-in-the-Blank. Supply the missing word(s) or term(s) to complete the sentence.

1. A _____ _____ is a group of individuals who organize to win elections, to operate the government, and to determine public policy.

2. The first _____political division in the U. S. occurred before the adoption of the Constitution.

3. The _____ Party is the oldest continuing political party in the western world.

4. The American political party that emerged in the late 1850s from the remains of the Whig Party is the

    _____ _____.

5. Each layer in the formal structure of a political party is _____from the other layers.

6. The real strength and power of a national party is at the _____ level.

7. The national chairperson of the party is selected during the _____ _____.

8. The period from the Civil War to the 1920s has been called one of _____ _____

9. The Democrat party has been known in modern times as the party of _____ , _____

    classes, and _____ groups.

10. Most enduring third parties have had a strong _____foundation.

True/False. Circle the appropriate letter to indicate if the statement is true or false.

1. T   F   Cadre is the name for the nucleus of party activists that carry out major party functions.
2. T   F   American political parties are tightly organized pyramid-shaped organizations with the
             national chairperson dictating policy to lower levels.
3. T   F   The party platform is largely ignored once a party captures control of the government.
4. T   F   The national chairperson of each major party is actually chosen by the party's presidential
             nominee.
5. T   F   The Federal Election Commission (FEC) rules for campaign financing place restrictions on
             third-party candidates.
6. T   F   The general public feels that the Democrats handle foreign policy better than the Republicans.
7. T   F   All counties and states in the United States use the plurality, winner-take-all electoral system.
8. T   F   The most successful third party in the U.S. was the Socialist Party under the leadership of
             Eugene Debs.
9. T   F   Minor parties have not played an important role in American politics.
10. T   F   It appears that the electorate is increasingly voting a straight ticket.

Multiple-Choice. Circle the correct response.

1. The main feature differentiating a faction from a political party is that a faction
    a. includes only conservatives, while a political party may have both liberals and conservatives.
    b. generally does not have a permanent organized structure.
    c. works best if there are competing factions in opposition to it.
    d. helps to extend democracy to the rank-and-file party member.

2. Political parties in the United States tend to perform all of the following activities except

    a. recruit candidates for public office.

    b. organize and run elections.

    c. act as the organized opposition to the party in power.

    d. establish a large cadre of highly disciplined dues-paying party members.

3. The first two opposing groups in United States politics were the

    a. Democrats and Republicans.

    b. Federalists and Anti-Federalists.

    c. Washingtonians and Jeffersonians.

    d. Independents and Whigs.

4. The era from 1816 to 1828 when attention was centered on the character of the individual running for office rather than on party identification is referred to as the era of

    a. good feeling.

    b. factional politics.

    c. personal politics.

    d. democratic politics.

5. After the end of the Civil, the _____ became heavily Democratic, and the _____ became heavily Republican.

    a. North-South.

    b. South-North.

    c. East-West.

    d. West-East.

6. The modern party constituencies were created from the

    a. Post-Civil War period.

    b. Progressive Movement.

    c. New Deal period.

    d. Vietnam protest period.

7. The main purpose of the national party conventions every four years is to

    a. nominate the presidential and vice-presidential candidates.

    b. write a party platform.

    c. check the credentials of all party activists.

    d. develop a strategy for the upcoming presidential election.

8.   In terms of party organization, the real strength and power of the Democratic and Republican parties

   a.   reside with their members in the U.S. Congress.

   b.   lie with their national committee chairpersons.

   c.   reside at the state level of party organization.

   d.   are determined by the number of election victories each party achieves in a given time period

9.   The principal organizing structure for each political party at the state level is the

   a.   precinct committee.

   b.   ward captain.

   c.   state central committee.

   d.   governor's council.

10.   Rewarding members of a political party with government jobs and/or contracts is known as

   a.   bribery.

   b.   graft and corruption.

   c.   non-competitive bidding.

   d.   patronage.

11.   Since the presidency of Franklin D. Roosevelt, the core of the Democratic Party has been

   a.   middle-class, working Americans.

   b.   upper-class liberals.

   c.   minorities, the working class, and ethnic groups.

   d.   middle to upper-class Protestants and independents

12.   The pursuit of political interests of special concern to a region of the country is

   a.   sectional politics.

   b.   special politics.

   c.   dirty politics.

   d.   federal politics.

13.   The major disagreement in American politics has been over _____ issues.

   a.   religious

   b.   social

   c.   foreign policy

   d.   economic

14.   The most successful minor parties have been those that have

   a.   focused on the positive things in life, not the negative.

   b.   been formed from the break-up of the Democratic party prior to WWI.

   c.   split from major parties.

   d.   opposed the existing economic power structure.

15. Which of the following statement about party identification is true?

    a.   In recent years, Democrats have increased, while Republicans and Independents have decreased.

    b.   In recent years, Independents have increased, while Democrats and Republicans have decreased.

    c.   In recent years, Republicans have increased, while Democrats and Independents have decreased.

    d.   In recent years, Democrats, Republicans, and Independents have decreased.

Short Essay Questions. Briefly address the major concepts raised by the following questions.

1. Distinguish among a political party, interest group, and faction.

2. Trace the evolution of political party development within the United States.

3. Identify the formal structure of political party organization in America.

4. Discuss the reasons for the two-party system in the United States.

ANSWERS TO THE PRACTICE EXAM

Fill-in-the-Blank.

1. political party [p. 275]

2. partisan [p. 277]

3. Democratic [p. 279]

4. Republican Party [p. 279]

5. autonomous [p. 282]

6. state [p. 285]

7. national convention [p. 284]

8. sectional politics [p. 291]

9. minorities, working, ethnic [p. 288]

10. ideological [p. 296]

True/False

1. T [p. 276]	3. F [p. 282]	5. T [p. 294]	7. F [p. 294]	9. F [p. 298]
2. F [p. 282]	4. T [p. 284]	6. F [p. 289]	8. T [p. 296]	10. F [p. 299]

Multiple-Choice.

1. b [p. 275]	4. c [p. 278]	7. a [p. 282]	10. d [p. 285]	13. d [p. 293]
2. d [p. 276]	5. b [p. 279]	8. c [p. 285]	11. c [p. 288]	14. c [p. 296]
3. b [p. 277]	6. c [p. 280]	9. c [p. 285]	12. a [p. 291]	15. b [p. 299]

Chapter 9   Political Parties

Short Essay Answers. Briefly address the major concepts raised by the following questions.

1. Distinguish among a political party, interest group, and faction [p. 275].

    *   A political party is a group of political activists who organize to win elections, to operate the government, and to determine public policy.

    *   An interest group is a collection of individuals that attempts to influence elections, influence elected officials, and influence public policy.

    *   Factions are smaller groups, which may exist within political parties, and are trying to obtain certain benefits for themselves.

2. Trace the evolution of political party development within the United States [p. 277-280].

    *   The formation of political parties in the U.S. went through six basic periods. These are; (1) the creation of parties, (2) the era of personal politics, (3) the period of President Jackson to the Civil War, (4), the post-Civil War period, (5) the progressive period, and (6) the modern period.

    *   The first parties were created from 1789 to 1812 around support for ratifying the Constitution, the Federalists for ratification, the Anti-Federalists against.

    *   From 1816 to 1828, voters focused on the candidates rather than the parties.

    *   From 1828 to 1860, political parties tended to focus on Andrew Jackson, and the Democratic and Whig parties developed.

    *   The post-Civil War period of 1864 to 1892 created our current two-party system, as the anti-slavery Republican Party was created.

    *   The Progressive era from 1896 to 1928 led to the split in the Republican Party and the election of the Democrats in 1912, which enacted much of the Progressive Party platform.

    *   The New Deal programs of President Franklin Roosevelt, which established the current political landscape of the political party system, created the modern period from 1932.

3. Identify the formal structure of political party organization in America [p. 282-287].

    *   The formal political party organization structure consists of the national level, the state level and the local level. See the theoretical structure of political parties, Figure 9-2 page 282.

    *   The national party organization consists of a national convention held every four years. At this convention, the party selects its candidates for president and vice-president, writes a party platform, selects a national committee, and selects a national chairperson.

    *   The state central committee will carry out the decisions of the state party convention, and in some states, direct the activities of the state chairperson.

    *   The local party organization called the grass roots uses county committees and their chairpersons to direct and assist the activities of precinct leaders.

4. Discuss the reasons for the two-party system in the United States [p. 291-294].

   - The historical foundations of the two-party system developed around relatively distinct sets of issues.
   - The first of these issues was ratifying the Constitution, which led to the Federalists and Anti-Federalists.
   - Political socialization, in which parents influence their children's choice of political party, continued the two-party system.
   - The American political culture emphasizes the commonality of goals, which makes the two parties broad and able to accommodate different viewpoints.
   - The winner-take-all election system makes it very difficult for third parties to win elections.
   - State and federal election laws make it difficult for third parties to get on the ballot.

Chapter 10
Campaigns, Candidates, And Elections

CHAPTER SUMMARY

The People Who Run for Political Office

People who run for political office can be divided into two groups; those who are "self-starters," and those who are recruited [p. 307]. There are few constitutional requirements for federal office.

- A President must be a natural-born citizen, age 35, and a resident of the U.S for fourteen years when sworn in [p. 308].
- A Vice-President must meet the same requirements as President but cannot be a resident of the same state.
- A Senator must be a citizen for nine years, 30 years old, and a resident of the state from which he/she is elected.
- A Representative must be a citizen for seven years, 25 years old, and a resident of the state from which he/she is elected.

While these requirements are minimal, most current office holders are white males, largely because of past discrimination. Women, however, have made tremendous gains in the last 10 years. See Figure 10-1, page 309, for a look at the number of women candidates elected. Most candidates elected to office tend to be professionals, especially lawyers [p. 310].

The Modern Campaign Machine

American political campaigns are extravagant year-long events that cost a total of several billion dollars in 1998. Since the 1960s, most candidates hire a professional, paid, political consultant to run their campaigns [p. 311-312].

The Strategy of Winning

The goal of every political campaign is to win the election. An important concerns is how well-known the candidate is. The problem of name recognition is obviously a problem for a third party candidate, because they do not have the Democrat or Republican name to run on [p. 313]. Most candidates will use two major strategies in the campaign: polls and focus groups. Polls give the candidate information about the voters' views, and as the election approaches, tracking polls indicate how well the campaign is going. Focus groups allow the candidate to gain insights into the public's perception of the candidate [p. 314].

Where Does the Money Come From?

The tremendous cost of political campaigns has caused concern among the public and led Congress to pass a number of laws to attempt to regulate campaign financing. Beginning in 1925, the Corrupt Practices Acts were passed but proved largely ineffective. The Hatch Act in 1939 attempted to limit spending by political groups, but was also easily evaded [p. 315]. The Federal Election

Campaign Act of 1972 and 1974 essentially replaced all past laws and instituted a major reform. These laws created the Federal Election Commission (FEC), provided public funding for presidential elections, put limits on presidential spending, limited campaign contributions, and required disclosure by candidates [p. 316].

Within a few years of these laws, three major loopholes appeared to evade the new campaign financing laws [p. 317-319]..

- soft money—given to political parties rather than a candidate
- independent expenditures—money given to help a candidate, but not part of his campaign funds
- bundling—adding together maximum contributions to influence a candidate

Running for President: The Longest Campaign

The American presidential election has two distinct phases. The first begins in January with the first presidential primary and ends in June with the party's national convention. The second phase usually begins on Labor Day, and culminates in the presidential election in November [p. 320]. After the 1968 Democratic National Convention changes in the primary election system, candidates realized that primary elections could be a springboard to winning the presidency. A candidate who wins the first caucus in Iowa and the first primary in New Hampshire is labeled a front-runner by the media and receives a big campaign boost [p. 322].

Other states, attempting to get the media coverage, and influence the presidential nomination, began to move up the day of their primary elections. This practice is known as front-loading [p. 323]. A number of southern states moved their primaries to the same day, which became known as Super Tuesday. The national convention is the end result of all the state primary elections. In recent years, the delegates selected in the primaries have already given the nomination to a candidate before the convention begins. This has lessened the interest and media coverage of the national convention.

The Electoral College

The Constitution created the Electoral College as the official method of electing a president. Each state is responsible for choosing electors who will officially vote for president. The number of a state's electoral votes is based on the number of a state's Senators and Representatives. The total number of electors in the Electoral College is 538. It requires 270 electoral votes to be elected president. See Figure 10-2, page 325, for each state's electoral votes. A plurality of voters in a state chooses one slate of electors who are pledged to vote on the first Monday after the second Wednesday in December in the state capital for the president and vice president. The ballots are counted and certified before a joint session of Congress early in January. See Figure 10-3, page 326, for a view of the overall process. This process has been criticized for a number of reasons:

- a candidate could win the popular vote, but lose the electoral vote.

- states with small electoral votes are ignored in the presidential campaign but get more electoral votes for fewer people.

The major reforms of the system have been suggested:

- direct election of the president
- require electors to vote for the candidate who won a plurality in the state [p.327].

How Are Elections Conducted?

The United States uses the secret or Australian ballot, which is prepared, distributed, and counted by government officials at public expense. There are two types of ballots, the office-block, which focuses on the office rather than the party, and the party-column, which focuses on the party rather than the office. In recent years, registering and voting have been available through the mail. Experts are divided over whether voting by mail increases participation or only increases the opportunity for fraud [p. 328].

Voting in National, State, and Local Elections

Voter turnout in the United States in the 1996 presidential election was only 48.8 percent of eligible voters. This placed the U.S. last among selected democratic nations in voter turnout. See Figure 10-4, page 329, for the list of countries. There are two theories about the decline of voter turnout in the U.S. One is that the decline is a threat to our democracy. The other is that people are basically satisfied with the status quo, and, therefore, don't vote. Studies show that there are a number of factors that seem to influence voting turnout. These factors are age, education, minority status, income, and two-party competition. Voters tend to be older, more educated, wealthy, not from an ethnic minority, and living in an area of two-party competition versus one party's dominance. See Table 10-3 and 10-4, page 331, for a look at different turnout rates. Political scientists believe that people don't vote because

- voters have been withdrawing politically
- people choose not to learn about issues because they believe their votes will not make a difference—a circumstance called the rational ignorance effect [p. 332].

Legal Restrictions on Voting

Historically, only white males who owned property were allowed to vote. The Constitution allowed the states to decide who should vote. Since the Civil War, Constitutional Amendments and acts of Congress, such as the Voting Rights Act, have extended the right to vote. Voting requires registration, and some scholars believe that even the minimal requirements of citizenship, age, and residency keep some people from voting [p. 334].

How Do Voters Decide?

The factors that influence voters' decisions are socioeconomic, demographic, and psychological. Socioeconomic and demographic factors include education, income and socioeconomic status, religion, ethnic background, gender, age, and geographic region. See Table 10-5 on pages 336-337 for a view of how these factors influence voting in selected presidential election years. A discussion of these factors continues to page 339. Psychological factors include party identification, the image or perception of the candidate, and issues, particularly economic issues [p. 340].

Campaigns, Candidates, and Elections: Issues for the New Century

The length and cost of political campaigns will continue to be issues of concern. The most pressing issue for the future seems to be the increasingly high level of cynicism in voters, which may be a major factor in the low levels of participation in all governmental elections.

KEY TERMS

Australian ballot—p. 327

caucus—p. 322

corrupt practices act—p. 315

elector—p. 325

front-loading—p. 323

Hatch Act—p. 315

independent expenditures—p. 317

office-block ballot—p. 328

party-column ballot—p. 328

plurality—p.325

presidential primary—p. 320

rational ignorance effect—p. 332

socioeconomic status—p. 336

soft money—p. 317

tracking polls—p. 314

voter turnout—p. 329

CD-ROM *AMERICA AT ODDS*

VOTER APATHY. The module for Chapter 10 looks at reasons why eligible voters don't vote. While suffrage has been expanded—note the 1993 Motor Voter Act, which made registering to vote easier—about 40% of the eligible voters in the U.S. are not registered. They cite being "too busy" or disinterested or alienated from politics. About 60% of unregistered voters would consider themselves Democrats. About two-thirds of the American public agrees that it is the duty of a citizen to vote. A ten-question interactive multiple-choice quiz allows you to reinforce key points about the material presented.

PRACTICE EXAM

(Answers appear at the end of this chapter.)

Fill-in-the-Blank. Supply the missing word(s) or term to complete the sentence.

1.   In terms of gender and race, holders of political office in the U.S. are overwhelmingly _____ _____.

2.   Candidates who run for office are either "self-starters" or _____.

3.   Campaign leadership has changed from volunteer campaign managers to paid _____.

4.   Campaign contributions that escape the limits of federal election laws are called _____ _____.

5.   Candidates use focus groups and _____ _____ to evaluate their campaigns.

6.   The number of a state's electors in the Electoral College equals the state's total number of _____

and _____ in the U.S. Congress.

7.   A _____ _____ is a form of general election ballot in which the candidates are

arranged in one column under their respective party names and symbols.

8.   Citizenship, age, and _____ are the requirements to register to vote.

9.   The higher the income, the more likely a person is to vote for the _____ Party.

10. With the possible exception of race, _____ _____ has most determined a

person's vote in national elections.

True/False. Circle the appropriate letter to indicate if the statement is true or false.

1.   T   F   When campaigning for public office, candidates are depending more and more upon the
             resources of their political parties.

2.   T   F   Political campaigns seem to be getting longer and more excessive each year.

3.   T   F   Tracking polls are used by the government to keep track of campaign contributions.

4.   T   F   Primary elections were instituted for the purpose of opening the nomination process to rank-
             and file party members.

5. T   F   In a process called front-loading, states changed the dates of their primaries to gain more influence over nominating presidential candidates.

6. T   F   The framers of the Constitution favored selection of the president and vice-president by the general population.

7. T   F   In general, the more education you have the more likely you are to vote.

8. T   F   Public funding of political campaigns is provided by law for all national elections.

9. T   F   Today, all states have uniform qualifications for voting and registration.

10. T   F   Historically, economic issues most strongly influence voters' choices.

Multiple-Choice. Circle the correct response.

1. The constitutional qualifications for the office of president include all of the following EXCEPT

    a.   natural born citizen.

    b.   years of age.

    c.   14-year resident of U.S.

    d.   registered voter.

2. Which of the following characteristics is not descriptive of a professional campaign?

    a.   increased length of campaign

    b.   paid political consultant

    c.   increased costs of campaign

    d.   increased use of volunteers

3. The first attempt by Congress to regulate campaign spending was the

    a.   Hatch Act.

    b.   Corrupt Practices Acts.

    c.   CREEP Act.

    d.   Federal Election Campaign Act.

4. The purpose of the Federal Election Commission is to

    a.   create an aura of good feeling in federal elections.

    b.   oversee and enforce the provisions of the 1974 Federal Election Campaign Act.

    c.   scrutinize and attempt to discover loopholes in the 1974 Act.

    d.   oversee federal and state elections.

5. The group that now controls the nomination process for president is the

    a.   mass public.

    b.   party elites.

    c.   presidential nominees themselves.

    d.   mass media.

6. The framers of the constitution established the Electoral College because they wanted

    a.   to ensure the general population would have an opportunity to directly vote for president.

    b.   the choice of president and vice-president to be made by a few dispassionate, reasonable men.

    c.   only candidates for president and vice-president who had graduated from the Electoral College.

    d.   the political parties to be able to control the selection of president and vice-president.

7. The major parties are not in favor of eliminating the Electoral College because

    a.   the electors are always influential party members, who might be offended.

    b.   the major party candidates would not receive as much public funding.

    c.   the masses are not capable of making this important decision.

    d.   they fear it would give minor parties a more influential role in the election outcome.

8. The form of ballot that encourages straight-ticket voting is the

    a.   closed ballot.

    b.   open ballot.

    c.   office-block ballot.

    d.   party-column ballot.

9. The coattail effect

    a.   appears only in national elections.

    b.   refers to voting by mail.

    c.   describes the influence of the candidate who is at the top of the ballot.

    d.   is an aspect of voter fraud.

10. Which statement is correct with respect to age as a factor in voting?

    a.   Age is not a significant factor in voting.

    b.   Younger voters tend to turn out in higher percentages than older voters.

    c.   Turnout increases the older the age group until the age of 65 and older.

    d.   Younger voters have more enthusiasm for voting than older voters.

11. As a factor in voting, more education seems to correlate with

    a.   voting Republican.

    b.   voting Democratic.

    c.   voting independent.

    d.   disillusionment and apathy.

12. Since their introduction in the late nineteenth century, voter registration laws have

    a.   increased the numbers of voters.

    b.   reduced the voting of African-Americans and immigrants.

    c.   created a new class of active and committed voters.

    d.   allowed the manipulation of election results by party bosses.

13. If we measure the influence of socioeconomic status by profession, then

   a.   skilled tradesman tend to vote independently.

   b.   unskilled workers tend to vote more than skilled workers do.

   c.   those of higher socioeconomic status tend to vote Republican.

   d.   those of higher socioeconomic status tend to vote Democratic.

14. With the possible exception of race, the biggest determinant of voting in national elections is

   a.   religion.

   b.   age.

   c.   party identification.

   d.   income.

15. Historically, the issues that have the strongest influence on voters' choices have been

   a.   religious.

   b.   foreign policy issues.

   c.   environmental issues.

   d.   economic issues.

Short Essay Questions. Briefly address the major concepts raised by the following questions.

1. Explain the legislative action taken to reform campaign financing.

2. Describe the presidential election process from primaries to the general election.

3. Discuss the Electoral College procedures and proposed reforms.

4. Describe and explain the factors associated with voting.

ANSWERS TO THE PRACTICE EXAM

Fill-in-the-Blank.

1. white, male [p. 309]

2. recruited [p. 307]

3. political consultant [p. 311]

4. soft money [p. 317]

5. tracking polls [p. 314]

6. senators, representatives [p. 325]

7. party-column [p. 328]

8. residency [p. 334]

9. Republican [p. 337]

10. party identification [p. 340]

True/False

| 1. F [p. 311] | 3. F [p. 314] | 5. T [p. 323] | 7. T [p. 331] | 9. F [p. 334] |
| 2. T [p. 311] | 4. T [p. 320] | 6. F [p. 325] | 8. T [p. 316] | 10. F [p. 340] |

Multiple Choice.

1. d [p. 308]	4. b [p. 316]	7. d [p. 327]	10. c [p. 331]	13. c [p. 337]
2. d [p. 311]	5. a [p. 321]	8. d [p. 328]	11. a [p. 331]	14. c [p. 340]
3. b [p. 315]	6. b [p. 325]	9. c [p. 328]	12. b [p. 335]	15. b [p. 340]

Short Essay Answers. Briefly address the major concepts raised by the following questions.

1. Explain the legislative action taken to reform campaign financing [p. 315-319].
   - Congress in 1925 passed the Corrupt Practices Acts, which were largely ineffective.
   - The Hatch Act, passed in 1939, put limits on the amount of money that political groups could contribute to political campaigns.
   - The Federal Election Campaign Act of 1972 replaced the past laws and instituted a major reform.
   - After the Watergate scandal, the Federal Election Campaign Act of 1974 created more reform that:
     ◊ created the Federal Election Commission.
     ◊ provided public funding for presidential primaries and general elections.
     ◊ limited presidential campaign spending.
     ◊ limited contributions
     ◊ required disclosure.
   - 1976 Amendments to the law allowed for the creation of Political Action Committees.
   - These laws cans be avoided by the use of soft money, independent expenditures, and bundling.

2. Describe the presidential election process from primaries to the general election [p. 320-324].
   - The presidential election process divides into two different campaigns from January to November linked together by the political party's national conventions.
   - The presidential primary system begins with the Iowa caucus in January and New Hampshire primary in February. The winner of these elections is dubbed the front-runner by the media, which gives that candidate a big boost in their campaign.
   - In a process known as front-loading, states have moved up their primary dates to gain more influence in the nomination of presidential candidates. California has moved its primary to March. Southern states hold their primaries on the same date known as Super Tuesday.
   - The caucuses and primaries select delegates who go to the national convention. The main purpose of the national convention is to nominate the president and vice-president.
   - The president and vice-president nominees begin their campaigns around Labor Day.

3. Discuss the Electoral College procedures and proposed reforms [p. 325-327].

    • Under the Constitution, the Electoral College elects the president and vice-president.

    • Each state's electors are chosen during the presidential election year. Each state's number of electors equals its number of senators (two) plus its number of representatives. See Figure 10-2, page 325, for the number of electors for each state. See Figure 10-3 for the Electoral College process.

    • It takes 270 electoral votes, out of 538, to win the presidency.

    • The two major suggested reforms of the Electoral College are:

        ◊ elect the president by popular vote

        ◊ require each elector by law to vote for the candidate who received the plurality in the elector's state.

4. Describe and explain the factors that affect voting behavior.

    • There is an established relationship between voting participation and the following factors: age, educational level, minority status, income level, and the existence of two-party competition.

    • Young people vote in the lowest percentages. The voting turnout increases with each age group until 65 years and over. See Table 10-3, page 331.

    • The more education people have, the more likely they are to vote. The voting turnout increases with each level of education until college graduation. See Table 10-4, page 331.

    • Wealthier people tend to vote in higher numbers. People with annual family incomes of $50, 000 or more are twice as likely to vote as people with annual family incomes of under $15, 000.

    • States that have competitive two-party elections have higher turnout rates.

Chapter 11
The Media

CHAPTER SUMMARY

The Media's Functions

The mass media performs six functions in U.S. society.

- entertaining—media devote the most time to entertainment and, sometimes, stimulate discussion of important issues by presenting them in dramatic form.

- reporting the news—a primary function of the media in a democratic society

- identifying public problems—a crucial role that helps to set the public agenda

- socializing new generations—the content of media, particularly television, offers children and immigrants a view of the basic American values

- providing a political forum—offers citizens a way to participate in the public debate

- making profits—the various media are privately owned businesses. This makes for a complex relationship and balance among public opinion, government, and the media [p. 349-351].

History of the Media in the United States

The earliest medium in the United States was the newspaper. Some historians feel that the print media played an important role in unifying the country. Many of these early newspapers were politically sponsored [p. 252]. In the nineteenth century, the high-speed rotary press and the telegraph made possible the publication of mass-readership newspapers; as competition among these newspapers grew, a sensationalistic, irresponsible journalism, called yellow journalism, developed [p. 353]. In 1920, the first scheduled radio broadcast transmitted the returns of the 1920 presidential election. This was the beginning of broadcast media, radio and television [p. 354]. Today, cable, satellite television, and the Internet have made possible narrow casting, or targeting small sectors of the audience. Literally thousands of talk shows on radio, television, and Internet have recently arisen [p. 355-356].

The Primacy of Television

Television is the most influential medium. The use of images conveys powerful content. The format of television tends to produce brief memorable comments called sound bites that can easily fit into a news broadcast. Sound bites may have increased the impact of television on political events [p. 358].

The Media and Political Campaigns

For political candidates, advertising is one of the most effective uses of mass media. Perhaps the most influential political ad of all time was the "Daisy Girl" ad used by President Johnson against Barry Goldwater in the 1968 presidential election. After this advertisement appeared, the concept of negative advertising came to occupy a major portion of many political campaigns. Political advertising is the most costly expenditure in a political campaign, so candidates have attempted to turn the news media's free to their advantage. Political campaign advisers, called spin-doctors, attempt to interpret campaign-event news in a way positive to the candidate. This is referred to as putting spin on a story or event. Televised presidential debates have become a feature of the presidential elections since the 1960 debate between John Kennedy and Richard Nixon. Candidates soon realized that the image they presented on television was critical to their political campaigns.   The question of how much influence all this media coverage has on voters is hard to answer, because of the many factors that influence how someone votes. Studies tend to indicate that media have the biggest impact on voters who are truly undecided about their choices [p. 359-363].

The Media and the Government

The mass media not only influences political campaigns, but it influences government and government officials. The president has a love-hate relationship with the media. The White House press corps attempt to discover news about the president, and the president's press secretary tries to reveal only the information that the president wantsthe press to have. The media and the president need each other to survive. Perhaps no president was as successful at surviving the media than Ronald Reagan, who was called the "great communicator." The media also play a big role in setting the public agenda. Although the media does not decide the agenda, they do raise various issues for discussion and resolution [p. 363-367].

Government Regulation of the Media

Although the United States has the freest press in the world, regulation of media does exist. Electronic media, which did not exist when the Constitution was written, has been regulated more than print media. The Federal Communication Commission (FCC) was created to regulate broadcast media. In the 1996 Telecommunications Act, Congress opened up the telephone, television, and Internet industries to vast mergers. The question for the future is how to prevent the giant telecommunication companies of today from becoming giant monopolies. In general, the broadcasting industry has avoided government regulation of content by establishing it own code. There has been increasing debate about banning the broadcast of polls and early predications of winners in presidential elections. This "early calling" of elections has seemed to influence the outcome of elections. The Telecommuni-cation Act of 1996 included two provisions designed to control the content of electronic media. One provision required television manufacturers to put a "V-chip" in each set to allow parents to block television programs. The other provision attempted to regulate content on the Internet. This provision was ruled unconstitutional by the Supreme Court in 1997 [p.367-368].

The Public's Right to Media Access

Both the Federal Communication Commission and the courts have supported the concept that citizens have a right of access to media. The airwaves are public and the government can dictate to the private companies how to use these airwaves. Technology in the form of the Internet is giving citizens more and more access [p. 369].

Bias in the Media

Many studies have attempted to determine if there is a recognizable bias in media. For years, it was assumed that there was a bias toward the liberal ideology. Recently, the bias seems to have slipped more to the conservative ideology. In Thomas Patterson's view, reported in his recent book, the bias of media is actually to emphasize bad news and cynicism rather than any political position [p. 370].

The Media and Politics: Issues for the New Century

The Internet has created literally thousands of site to allow citizens to "chat" with each other, journalists, and politicians. The intensity of these conversations seems to indicate that Americans are eager to use this new technology to invigorate our democracy [p. 371].

KEY TERMS

bias—p. 370

electronic media—p. 355

managed news—p. 353

media access—p. 369

narrow casting—p. 355

press secretary—p. 363

public agenda—p. 350

sound bite—p. 358

spin—p. 360

spin doctor—p. 360

White House press corps—p. 363

yellow journalism—p. 354

CD-ROM *AMERICA AT ODDS*

NEGATIVE ADVERTISING.   One interactive module for Chapter 11 looks at the two greatest negative campaign ads in U.S. history, the "Daisy Girl" ad in the 1964 presidential campaign and the "Willie Horton" ad in the 1988 presidential campaign. The module traces the history of negative advertising throughout American political campaigns. Finally, you can see video clips of two negative campaign commercials. A ten-question interactive multiple-choice quiz reinforces key points in the material.

FREE TV TIME FOR POLITICIANS.   A second module for Chapter 11 focuses on the characteristics of political advertising. The history of proposals for free TV time is presented, followed by pro and con arguments, and, finally, an interactive exercise: you can be a lobbyist representing the broadcast industry on this issue. A ten-question interactive multiple-choice quiz reinforces key points in the material.

NEWS FROM THE NET.   A third module for Chapter 11 looks at key issues of the latest medium, the Internet. The module begins with a discussion of how to gather and evaluate information from the Internet, followed by a brief history of the development of the Internet. The laws that apply to this new media are available, and finally, you test your Internet literacy in an interactive format. A ten-question interactive multiple-choice quiz reinforces key points in the material.

PRACTICE EXAM

(Answers appear at the end of this chapter.)

Fill-in-the-Blank. Supply the missing word(s) or term to complete the sentence.

1.   By far, the greatest number of radio and television hours is dedicated to _____.

2.   The primary goal of the mass media in all their forms is _____.

3. A term for sensationalistic, irresponsible journalism is _____.

4. Specialized programming by the media for specialized tastes is referred to as _____.

5. _____ is the most influential medium.

6. In television news coverage, a several-second comment selected or crafted for its immediate impact is

    referred to as a _____ _____.

7. An interpretation of campaign events or election results that is most favorable to a candidate's

    campaign strategy is referred to as the _____.

8. The person who represents the White House before the media is the _____ _____.

9. The government has greater control over the_____ media than the_____ media.

10. The FCC and the courts have ruled that _____ have a right of access to media.

True/False. Circle the appropriate letter to indicate if the statement is true or false.
1. T   F   Thomas Jefferson was a firm believer in control of the press by government.
2. T   F   Many historians believe that the print media played an important role in unifying the country.
3. T   F   Because of diversified cable broadcasting, television has become more like print media
             targeting specialized tastes.
4. T   F   Newspapers are the primary news source for the majority of Americans.
5. T   F   In general, challengers have much more to gain from debating than do incumbents.

6. T   F   It appears that the media are most influential with those who have not formed an opinion about political candidates or issues.

7. T   F   Studies indicate that the media does not play an important role in setting the public agenda.

8. T   F   The United States has the most highly regulated press in the world.

9. T   F   The government places fewer restrictions on the broadcast media than on the print media.

10. T   F   The government has a right to dictate use of the airwaves because the airwaves are public domain.

Multiple-Choice. Circle the correct response.

1. By far the greatest number of radio and television broadcast hours are devoted to

    a. news analysis.

    b. sport broadcasting.

    c. entertaining the public.

    d. educational programming.

2. Information generated and distributed by the government in such a way as to give government interests priority over the facts is referred to as (the)

    a. fairness doctrine.

    b. right-to-know rule.

    c. narrow casting.

    d. managed news.

3. In the last fifteen years, the type of media that has increased by the largest percentage is

    a. cable.

    b. network affiliates.

    c. PBS.

    d. independent stations.

4. The 1952 presidential campaign was the first to involve the use of

    a. political action committees.

    b. presidential preference primaries.

    c. radio in a meaningful way.

    d. television in a meaningful way.

5. The term narrow casting refers to

    a. presenting only one side of an issue.

    b. media programming for specialized tastes.

    c. a biased news report.

    d. presenting a narrow image to your readership.

6. The first network broadcast by electronic medium was in the

    a. 1920s.

    b. 1930s.

    c. 1940s.

    d. 1950s.

7. Negative advertising works well in political campaigning because

    a. voters do not want to hear good things about candidates.

    b. voters have selective attention for the candidates they support.

    c. negative ads cost less to produce.

    d. negative ads are more memorable than ones that praise the candidate's virtues.

8. An interpretation of campaign events that is most favorable to the candidate's position is called

    a. take.

    b. analysis.

    c. commentary.

    d. spin.

9. Studies have shown that

    a. the Internet will soon replace newspapers as the major source of news.

    b. radio talk-shows are now setting the public agenda.

    c. the media is losing its control over setting the public agenda.

    d. the media play an important part in setting the public agenda for government.

10. Studies suggest that the early announcement of election results based on exit polls

    a. has had a great effect on the election outcomes.

    b. has had a little effect on the election outcomes.

    c. has had the most effect on presidential elections.

    d. increases the interest of voters in the elections.

11. The Telecommunications Act of 1996 was an attempt to regulate

    a. radio talk shows.

    b. Hollywood movies.

    c. indecent materials on the Internet.

    d. violent professional sports on television.

12. Thomas E. Patterson's analysis of bias in the media indicates that the real bias in the news is

    a. a liberal bias.

    b. that it emphasizes bad news and cynicism.

    c. a conservative bias.

    d. that it emphasizes in-depth reporting over generalized coverage.

13. The "Daisy Girl" commercial form the 1964 presidential election campaign is a good example of

    a.   spin.

    b.   managed news.

    c.   negative advertising.

    d.   narrow casting.

14. The increasing dependence of campaigns and candidates on the media makes the present time an era of

    a.   symbolic politics and weakened political attachments.

    b.   strengthened political attachments for both the old and new.

    c.   realignment of media support for partisan causes.

    d.   opportunity for greater investigative reporting.

15. "Chat" rooms on the Internet have shown that Americans are

    a.   apathetic.

    b.   unable to understand the technology.

    c.   willing and eager to express political opinions.

    d.   talkative, but lacking in political opinions.

Short Essay Questions. Briefly address the major concepts raised by the following questions.

1. Describe the major functions performed by the mass media in our society.

2. Trace the historical development of media from the colonial period to modern times.

3. Discuss the role of the media in political campaigns.

4. Describe the issues involved in the government's effort to regulate mass media.

ANSWERS TO THE PRACTICE EXAM

Fill-in-the-Blank.

1.	entertaining [p. 349]	6.	sound bite [p. 358]
2.	reporting the news [p. 350]	7.	spin [p. 360]
3.	yellow journalism [p. 354]	8.	press secretary [p. 363]
4.	narrow casting [p. 355]	9.	electronic, printed [p. 367]
5.	Television [p. 358]	10.	citizens [p. 369]

True/False.

1.	F [p. 352]	3.	F [p. 355]	5.	T [p. 361]	7.	F [p. 366]	9.	F [p. 367]
2.	T [p. 352]	4.	F [p. 358]	6.	T [p. 362]	8.	F [p. 367]	10.	T [p. 367]

Multiple-Choice.

1. c [p. 349]	4. d [p. 355]	7. d [p. 360]	10. b [p. 369]	13. c [p. 359]
2. d [p. 353]	5. b [p. 355]	8. d [p. 360]	11. c [p. 369]	14. a [p. 370]
3. a [p. 356]	6. a [p. 354]	9. d [p. 366]	12. b [p. 370]	15. c [p. 370]

Short Essay Answers. Briefly address the major concepts raised by the following questions.

1. Describe the major functions performed by the mass media in our society [p. 349-351].

   The mass media performs 6 basic functions. These are:

   - Entertainment, which garners the most radio and television time
   - Reporting the news, a primary function for all forms of media.
   - Identifying public problems, setting the public agenda for the government.
   - Socializing new generations, teaching young children and immigrants about American core values.
   - Providing a political forum for public information and political campaigns— for candidates and public officials, as well as the generalpublic.
   - Making profits. The media in the United States are privately owned, but publicly regulated.

2. Trace the historical development of media from the colonial period to modern times [p. 352-358].

   - The first medium was small, politically sponsored newspapers that historians feel had an important role in unifying the country.
   - The high-speed rotary press and telegraph produced newspapers for general readership, the first mass media. These papers often indulged in sensational biased journalism known as yellow journalism.
   - The electronic media began with the broadcast over radio of the 1920 presidential election returns.
   - Television was first used in a significant way in the 1952 presidential election. Television has become the most influential and dominant medium.
   - New trends in mass media, such as radio talk shows, cable and satellite television, and the Internet pose a real challenge to the dominance of network television.

3. Discuss the role of the media in political campaigns [p. 358-362].

   - Media has made an obvious impact during political campaigns.
   - One of the most effective political ads of all time was the "Daisy Girl" ad in the 1964 presidential campaign. This ad was the beginning of the negative ad campaign, which is so effective because views tend to remember these kinds of ads.
   - The high cost of political ads has produced a need for a special media advisor to help candidates use or manage free news coverage to their advantage. These advisors are called spin-doctors, and the way that they interpret the news in favor of their candidates is called spin.

- Presidential debates have been a staple of the political campaigns since the 1960 election. Image on television has become a key concern of all candidates.

- The media's impact on elections is hard to measure, but it seems to have the greatest impact on the undecided voter.

4. Describe the issues involved in the government's effort to regulate mass media [p. 367-369].

   - The strong First Amendment protection of print media has not been provided to electronic media for a number of reasons.

   - The Federal Communication Commission was created to regulate electronic media.

   - The Telecommunication Act of 1996 ended the FCC rules that kept telephone companies from entering other kinds of communication businesses.

   - The government has influenced the content of the broadcast media by encouraging the use of codes or standards of content. Provisions of the Telecommunication Act of 1996 required a television "V-chip" to help parents' control their children's viewing, and attempted to regulate pornography on the Internet. The federal courts ruled that the provisions of the law applying to the Internet were unconstitutional.

   - Both the FCC and the federal courts have ruled that the airwaves are public property, and that the public has a basic right to media access.

Chapter 12
The Congress

CHAPTER SUMMARY

Why was Congress Created?

The framers of the American Constitution believed that the bulk of government power should be in the hands of the legislative branch. Large and small state imbalance was resolved at the Constitutional Convention by the creation of a bicameral Congress: representation based on population in the House; equal representation in the Senate. The differences between the two houses in this bicameral congress were further emphasized by a two-year term for Representatives and a six-year term for Senators [p. 379-380].

The Powers of Congress

The first seventeen clauses of Article I, Section 8 of the constitution specify most of the enumerated powers of Congress. Beyond these specific powers is the "necessary and proper" clause, which has allowed the power of the national government to expanded [p.380-381].

The Functions of Congress

Congress has six basic functions:

- lawmaking—the most obvious and important function of Congress. The idea for most legislation comes from outside, but Congress is solely responsible for approving legislation.
- service to constituents—accomplished by acting as an ombudsperson and doing casework. Service to constituents is an important aspect of getting re-elected.
- representation— a member can represent his or her constituency by being
  - ◊ a trustee who uses personal judgement
  - ◊ an instructed delegate who uses the constituents' judgement
  - ◊ a politico who uses both approaches depending on the issue
- oversight—to make sure that the laws are enforced and administered the way in which they were intended
- public education—an important part of helping to set the public agenda; primarily occurs in conunction with the media (ee Chapter 11).
- conflict resolution—devise compromises over issues arising out of scarce resources or differences in ideology [p. 381-384].

House-Senate differences

Congress is composed of two very different but co-equal chambers. Because it represents the population of the United States, the House is much larger at 435 members. Composed of two senators from each of the fifty states, the Senate has 100 members. See Table 12-1, page 385, which shows the major

differences between the House and the Senate. The size difference requires the House to have a Rules
Committee to limit debate, while the Senate has unlimited debate, sometimes leading to filibustering.
The Senate, because of its smaller number and greater powers from the Constitution, is considered the
more prestigious of the institutions [p. 386].

Congresspersons and the Citizenry: A Comparison

Members of Congress are more likely to be white, male, Protestant, and trained in higher-status
occupations, than the average citizen is. See Table 12-2 on page 387.

Congressional Elections

The process of electing a member of Congress varies according to the election laws of the state from
which he or she is elected. Many congressional candidates are self-starters and have ties to the local
district. In recent years, the costs of campaigns have escalated [p. 388-389]. Two major issues
influence congressional elections. These are

- a presidential election year, which can produce a "coattails" or a negative effect

- the power of incumbency, which makes it difficult for a challenger to defeat the office holder.

Office holders have greater name recognition, can claim credit for government programs, or take
positions on popular issues [p. 391]. See Table 12-4 page 390 for statistics on the power of
incumbency. In spite of the advantage of incumbency, in 1994 voters swept out the Democratic
majority in both chambers of Congress. This development while Democrat Bill Clinton is president,
created a period of "divided government" that will continue at least until the 2000 elections [p. 393].

Congressional Reapportionment

Because representation in the House is based on population, the 10-year census triggers a realignment
of the number of House seats with the latest population figures. This is called reapportionment. The
state legislatures redistrict or redraw political boundaries to match the changes that have occurred in the
populations of those districts [p. 393-394]. In the past, legislatures did not always carry out this
constitutional responsibility. In *Baker v. Carr* (1962), the Supreme Court ruled that this issue could
be reviewed by the court, and that the legislatures had to use the principle of "one person, one vote" to
redistrict. In *Reynolds v. Sims* (1964), the Court applied "one person, one vote" to both houses of the
state legislature, and in *Wesberry v. Sanders* (1964), applied it to Congress. One issue that has not
been resolved by the courts is gerrymandering, the manipulation of redistricting to give an advantage
to one political party. See Figure 12-1 and Figure 12-2 page 396 for examples of different types of
gerrymanders.

Pay, Perks, and Privileges

Members of Congress receive a salary of $136,700 a year, plus a number of benefits, such as free
parking, free medical care, generous pensions, liberal travel allowances, and free postage or franking
privileges. They are able to hire an extensive professional staff, and use the resources of the professional

staff of many other government agencies. Members of Congress are also exempt from certain laws that apply to the ordinary citizens [p. 397-398].

The Committee Structure

The committees and sub-committees of Congress perform most of the actual work of creating legislation in Congress. Committees are commonly known as "little legislatures" because the committee is a microcosm of what happens in the legislature [p. 399]. There are five types of committees [p. 400-401]:

- standing—permanent committees that oversee an area of legislative policy.

- select—operate for a limited time and a limited purpose

- joint—created to achieve agreement on legislation

- conference—a special joint committee

- the House Rules committee—unique to the House, necessary to set rules for 435 members

The leaders of House and Senate committees, called chairpersons, are selected by seniority among the members of the majority party in each chamber. See Table 12-5, page 400, for the names of the standing committees and chairs.

The Formal Leadership

The political parties organize the formal leadership of Congress.

- In the House, the Speaker, the Majority and Minority leaders, and party Whips provide leadership.
    - ◊ The Speaker of the House is the presiding officer of the House, a member of the majority party, and the most powerful member of the House [p. 402].
    - ◊ The Majority leader heads floor debate and cooperates with the Speaker
    - ◊ The Minority leader represents the minority party and speaks for the President if the minority party controls the White House.
    - ◊ Party officials called Whips assist the leaders in Congress.
- The formal leaders in the Senate are both ceremonial figures.
    - ◊ The Constitution established the Vice-President as the presiding officer or President of the Senate. The Vice-President is rarely present for a meeting of the Senate.
    - ◊ The Senate elects a President Pro Tempore ("pro tem") to preside in the absence of the Vice-President.
    - ◊ The real leadership power in the Senate is with the Majority and Minority floor leaders who are assisted by Whips.

See Table 12-6, page 404 for a complete list of the formal leadership structure in Congress

Chapter 12   The Congress

How Members of Congress Decide

It is difficult to define the factors that determine how a member of Congress will vote. The single best predictor of how a member will vote seems to be political party membership. Party membership can be influenced by cues from respected senior members, regional, and ideological differences [p. 405].

How a Bill Becomes Law

The process begins with a bill being introduced to the House or Senate or both. The bill is referred to the appropriate committee and subcommittee where the heart of the legislative process occurs. The content specialists on the committee closely examine the bill. If it is voted on favorably by the committee, the bill is sent to the Rules committee in the House or scheduled for floor debate in the Senate. The bill is debated and voted on by the entire House and Senate. If a bill has passed the House and Senate with a majority vote but in slightly different form, it will be sent to a conference committee to work out the differences in the bill. If approved by both the House and Senate, the bill is sent to the president for his signature or veto. See Figure 12-3 page 406, for an illustration of this entire process.

How Much Will the Government Spend?

The Constitution provides that all money bills originate in the House of Representatives. Congress requires that the president prepare and submit the executive budget to Congress for their approval. Budget conflicts with the president led Congress to pass the Budget and Impoundment Control Act in 1974. The federal government operates on a fiscal-year budget cycle that begins on October 1 each year. The Office of Management and Budget reviews each agency's budget request and prepares a budget, which the president submits to Congress in January of each year. Congress reviews the budget submitted by the president and, in May, determines the first budget resolution that establishes the overall budget spending. The second budget resolution, with the budget for each government agency, is supposed to be passed October 1. Often, Congress does not meet this deadline, and must pass a temporary law, called a continuing resolution, to keep government agencies open until the new budget can be agreed upon [p. 408-410]. See Figure 12-4, page 408 for an overview of the budget process.

The Questions of Congressional Ethics

Congressional ethics have been a serious issue for the voting public. Members of Congress have had a number of personal and financial scandals revolving around their use of unspent campaign funds for personal benefit. The public has developed a cynical view of Congress as an institution [p. 410].

The Congress: Issues for the New Century

The very cynical view which the public has of Congress seems to have fueled continued calls for term limits for members of Congress. The lack of women and minority representation in Congress is another issue that will face the institution in the 21st century.

KEY TERMS

bicameralism

conference committee

constituent

enumerated power

filibustering

fiscal year (fy)

gerrymandering

instructed delegate

oversight

politico

reapportionment

redistricting

seniority system

trustee

CD-ROM *AMERICA AT ODDS*

TERM LIMITS. The interactive module for Chapter 12 explores the issue of term limits for members of Congress. First trace the history of term limits from the days of the founding fathers, then view the arguments pro and con by political journalists, George Will and David Broder. Finally, you can use an interactive exercise to make up your own mind about the issue and reinforce key points.

PRACTICE EXAM

(Answers appear at the end of this chapter.)

Fill-in-the-Blank. Supply the missing word(s) or term(s) to complete the sentence.

1. The Founding Fathers believed that the bulk of the power exercised by the national government should

    be in the hands of the _____.

2. According to the framers of the Constitution, the House was to be the _____

    chamber and the Senate was to be the chamber of the _____.

3. A legislature that is divided into two separate assemblies is _____.

4. Most of the bills that Congress acts upon originate in the _____ _____.

5. _____ is the process by which congress reviews the laws it has enacted and ensures

    that they are being administered in the way Congress intended.

6. Under Senate Rule 22, debate may be ended by invoking _____.

7. The influence of a strong presidential candidate on the party's ballot is called _____.

8. _____ make up, by far, the largest occupational group among congresspersons.

9. Before the passage of the Seventeenth Amendment in 1913, senators were not elected by direct popular

    vote, but were appointed by _____ _____.

10. Committee Chairs in congress are selected by _____.

True/False. Circle the appropriate letter to indicate if the statement is true or false.
1. T   F   The founding fathers placed the bulk of national government power in the president's hands.
2. T   F   The principle function of any legislature is lawmaking.
3. T   F   Instructed delegates mirror the views of the majority of constituents who elected them.
4. T   F   The Rules Committee is the most powerful committee in the Senate.
5. T   F   Members of Congress must be cautious about what they say on the floor of Congress because
            of the danger of being sued for slander.
6. T   F   By far the most important committees in Congress are the standing committees.
7. T   F   Party membership is the single best predictor of a member's vote in Congress.
8. T   F   If Congress does not approve a budget by the beginning of the fiscal year, the government can
            continue to operate on continuing resolutions.
9. T   F   All money bills must originate in the House of Representatives.
10. T   F   Ethics is the most serious public relations problem confronting Congress today.

Multiple-Choice. Circle the correct response.

1.   The Senate is the chamber of the Congress that

      a.   must first approve all money bills.

      b.   must first approve amendments.

      c.   ratifies treaties.

      d.   has the first opportunity to override presidential vetoes.

2.   The voting behavior of an instructed delegate would represent the

      a.   majority view of his or her constituents.

      b.   broad interests of society.

      c.   interests of his or her party.

      d.   president in voting in Congress.

3.   Some functions are restricted to only one house of Congress. The Senate is the only house that can

      a.   propose amendments.

      b.   approve the budget.

      c.   approve presidential appointments.

      d.   investigate the president.

4.   The central difference between the House and the Senate is that the

      a.   House is much larger in membership than the Senate.

      b.   House represents people, the Senate represents geography.

      c.   Senate ratifies treaties.

      d.   House first appropriates money.

5.   The largest occupational group among congresspersons is

      a.   scientists.

      b.   business persons.

      c.   farmers.

      d.   lawyers.

6.   In the House of Rrepresentatives,

      a.   each state is allowed two representatives.

      b.   there is no set number of minimum or maximum for each state.

      c.   each state is allowed at least one representative.

      d.   membership from each state is determined by the House itself.

7. Most candidates for Congress must win the nomination for office in a

    a. party caucus.

    b. indirect primary.

    c. direct primary.

    d. party convention.

8. Mid-term Congressional elections

    a. attract as many voters as presidential elections.

    b. attract more voters than presidential elections.

    c. usually result in the president's party losing seats in Congress.

    d. usually result in the president's party gaining seats in Congress.

9. The Supreme Court cases of *Baker v. Carr*, *Reynolds v. Sims*, and *Wesberry v. Sanders* pertained to

    a. foreign policy.

    b. budget policy.

    c. reapportionment.

    d. campaign spending.

10. The Supreme Court first applied the principle of "one person, one vote" to congressional districts in

    a. *Baker v. Carr.*

    b. *Reynolds v. Sims.*

    c. *Wesberry v. Sander.s*

    d. *Plessy v. Ferguson.*

11. Gerrymandering refers to the process of

    a. ending debate in the Senate.

    b. redrawing legislative boundaries.

    c. forcing a bill out of committee.

    d. selecting a committee chair.

12. The phrase "little legislatures" refers to the

    a. legislatures that exist in the states.

    b. committees in Congress.

    c. departments of the federal bureaucracy.

    d. interest groups that lobby Congress.

13. The "third house of Congress" refers to

    a. standing committees.

    b. select committees.

    c. special committees.

    d. conference committees.

14.   In the House of Representatives, the majority leader

   a.   acts as spokesperson for the majority party in the House.

   b.   serves as Speaker of the House.

   c.   is elected in a vote of all the members of the House.

   d.   is rarely able to exert any meaningful leadership because of the dominance of the Speaker.

15.   The congressional budget process was very disjointed until the passage of the

   a.   Office of Management and Budget.

   b.   Budget and Impoundment Control Act.

   c.   Discharge Petition.

   d.   Council of Economic Advisers.

Short Essay Questions. Briefly address the major concepts raised by the following questions.

1.   Explain the major functions of Congress.

2.   Trace the development of congressional reapportionment.

3.   Describe the leadership positions in the House of Representatives and the Senate.

4.   Discuss the steps that a bill must take to become law.

ANSWERS TO THE PRACTICE EXAM

Fill-in-the-Blank.

1.   legislature [p. 379]

2.   common man's, elite [p. 379]

3.   bicameral [p. 379]

4.   executive branch [p. 381]

5.   Oversight [p. 383]

6.   cloture [p. 385]

7.   "coattails" [p. 389]

8.   Lawyers [p. 387]

9.   state legislatures [p. 388]

10.   seniority [p. 401]

True/False

1.   F [p. 379]   3.   T [p. 382]   5.   F [p. 398]   7.   T [p. 405]   9.   T [p. 405]

2.   T [p. 381]   4.   F [p. 385]   6.   T [p. 400]   8.   T [p. 409]   10.   T [p. 410]

Multiple Choice.

1. c [p. 380]   4. a [p. 384]   7. c [p. 389]   10. c [p. 393]   13. d [p. 401]

2. a [p. 382]   5. d [p. 387]   8. c [p. 389]   11. b [p. 395]   14. a [p. 403]

3. c [p. 380]   6. c [p. 388]   9. c [p. 393]   12. b [p. 399]   15. b [p. 408]

Short Essay Answers. Briefly address the major concepts raised by the following questions.

1. Explain the major functions of Congress [p. 381-383].

    •   There are six major functions of Congress, which include lawmaking, service to constituents, representation, oversight, public education, and conflict resolution.

    •   Lawmaking is the principal and most obvious function of a legislative body.

    •   Service to constituents is primarily carried out by doing casework and by acting as an ombudsperson with government agencies.

    •   A member of Congress can represent constituents by being a trustee, instructed delegate, or politico.

    •   The oversight function allows Congress to review laws enacted and ensure that they are being enforced and administered as intended.

    •   The public education function of Congress assists in agenda setting.

    •   Conflict resolution is a key function for government to resolve issues of scarce resources and differences in societal goals.

2. Trace the development of congressional reapportionment [p. 393-396].

    •   The process of reapportionment is the allocation of seats in the House of Representatives to each state after each census.

    •   The movement of people from rural areas to cities and suburbs created numerical mal-apportionment prior to 1960.

    •   In 1962, the Supreme Court in the case of *Baker v. Carr* ruled that the issue of reapportionment could be ruled on by the court on the basis of the "one person, one vote" principle.

    •   In 1964, the Supreme Court applied this principle to state legislatures in *Reynolds v. Sims*, and to congressional districts in *Wesberry v. Sanders*.

    •   Gerrymandering and "minority-majority" are issues of reapportionment that remain unresolved.

3. Describe the leadership positions in the House of Representatives and the Senate [p.402-404].

    •   See Table 12-6 page 404 for a complete list of the current individuals who hold leadership positions

    •   Leadership in the House consists of the Speaker, the majority and minority leaders and party whips.

    •   The Speaker is the most important leader in the House; he presides over the chamber, makes appointments, schedules legislation, decides points of order, and refers bills.

    •   The majority and minority leaders are elected in party caucus and act as spokespersons and leaders of their party.

    •   Whips are assistants to the party leaders.

- Leadership in the Senate consists of the vice-president, president pro tempore, majority and minority leaders, and party whips.
- The Constitution named the Vice-President as the ceremonial President of the Senate.
- The Senate elects a ceremonial leader, president pro tempore, to preside over the Senate in the vice-president's absence.
- The real leadership power in the Senate rests with the majority and minority leaders.
- Whips are assistants to Senate party leaders.

Discuss the steps that a bill must take to become law [p. 405-408].

- See Figure 12-3, page 406 for an illustration of the entire legislative process.
- The bill is introduced to the House or Senate or both.
- The bill is referred to the appropriate committee.
- The bill is referred to subcommittee.
- The full committee reports out the bill.
- The Rules Committee in the House establishes rules for the bill.
- The entire House debates the bill and vote on it.
- The same steps, except for the Rules Committee, occur in the Senate.
- Conference action may be required to clear up differences between the House and Senate.
- The bill goes to the president for approval or veto.

Chapter 13
The Presidency

CHAPTER SUMMARY

Who Can Become President?

To become president, a person must be

- a natural-born citizen,
- 35 years old
- a fourteen-year resident of the United States.

The informal requirements suggest the president will be an older (54), white, Protestant male [p. 419].

The Process of Becoming President

The voters do not vote directly for president and vice-president, but instead vote for electors who officially vote in the Electoral College. When the Electoral College has failed to elect a president, the House of Representatives has made the decision. The Twelfth Amendment adopted in 1804 clarified one aspect of this process by separating the election of the president and vice-president [p. 420].

The Many Roles of the President

The Constitution created five major roles or functions for the president:

- chief of state—a ceremonial role. See page 421 for a list of these activities.
- chief executive
  - ◊ the federal bureaucracy carries out many of the president's executive responsibilities
  - ◊ the president has appointive power to fill government office positions. See Table 13-1, page 423 for a list of these positions.
  - ◊ the president can grant reprieves and pardons for all federal crimes except impeachment
- commander-in-chief of the armed forces— represents civilian control of the military. Presidents have exercised more authority in this role than any other. In 1973, Congress attempted to gain more control over military actions by passage of the War Powers Resolution. Still, the powers of the president as commander-in-chief are extensive [p. 425].
- chief diplomat—the president has the power to recognize foreign governments, to make treaties subject to approval by the Senate, and to generally conduct United States foreign policy. Presidents have greatly expanded their power in foreign policy through the use of executive agreements that do not require Senate approval [p.427].
- chief legislator—represented in the annual State of the Union message and the power of the veto. The veto power was expanded to include a line-item veto on spending bills and was first used by President Clinton. Challenged in the case of *Clinton v. City of New York*, the line-item veto was ruled unconstitutional by the Supreme Court in 1998.

Other presidential powers are given to the president by statute from Congress, express powers, and inherent powers defined through practice [p. 433].

The President as Party Chief and Superpolitician

Although the Constitution mentions nothing about political party leadership, the President is head of his political party. A major tool of the president as party leader is patronage. The president must be concerned about three different constituencies: the public in general, the members of the political parties, and the Washington community. Approval ratings measure the president's success with these constituencies. See Figure 13-2, page 437 for a look at recent president's approval ratings.

The Special Uses of Presidential Power

Presidents have four special powers and privileges:

- emergency powers— the power to act in a crisis was first articulated by the Supreme Court in *United States v. Curtiss-Wright Export Corp* (1936) [p. 438].

- executive orders— have the force of law and must be published in the Federal Register

- executive privilege—the right of executive officials to withhold information from legislative committees on the basis of separation of powers. In *United States v. Nixon* (1974), the Supreme Court ruled that Nixon had to turn over the Watergate tapes because executive privilege could not be used to hide evidence in a criminal case. It is unclear how this concept will hold up under President Clinton's impeachment proceedings [p. 439].

- until recently, impoundment of funds—the right of the president to refuse to spend, or impound, funds allocated by Congress was ended by the Budget and Impoundment Control Act of 1974. The Supreme Court upheld this law in the case of *Train v. City of New York* (1975) [p. 441].

The Abuses of Executive Power and Impeachment

The constitution authorized the House to impeach, and the Senate to remove the president, vice-president, and other civil officials for "high Crimes and Misdemeanors." In the history of the United States, no president has been impeached and removed from office. President Andrew Johnson in 1868 was impeached and tried by the Senate, which failed to remove him by one vote. In 1974, the House Judiciary Committee recommended impeachment charges against President Nixon over the cover-up of the Watergate break-in. Nixon resigned the presidency before the full House voted impeachment charges. In 1998, the House Judiciary Committee recommended an impeachment inquiry against President Clinton over the cover-up of the Monica Lewinsky affair [p. 441-442].

The Executive Organization

At the beginning of Franklin Roosevelt's tenure as president, the executive staff numbered 37. Today, the staff is over 600. The advisory group for the president, called the cabinet, began with four officials. Today, there are 14 officials, including 13 secretaries of various departments and the Attorney General.

Modern presidents do not use the cabinet as an advisory group today, but prefer to rely on an informal group of advisers called the kitchen cabinet.

- In 1939, by executive order, President Franklin Roosevelt created the Executive Office of the President (EOP). The EOP consists of nine staff agencies that assist the president in carrying out all major duties. See pages 443-444 for a list of these agencies.

- One of the most important agencies in the EOP is the White House Office, which includes most of the key personnel and advisers to the president. In recent presidencies, the Chief of Staff is in charge of coordinating the White House Office.

- The Council of Economic Advisers (CEA) was created in 1946 to advise the president on economic matters.

- President Nixon created the Office of Management and Budget (OMB) from the Bureau of the Budget in 1970. This agency prepares the federal budget and advises the president on management techniques.

- The National Security Council brings together the foreign policy and military advisers to the president.

The Vice-Presidency

The only duty mandated by the Constitution calls for the vice-president to preside over the Senate and vote in the case of a tie vote. Traditionally, vice-presidents have been selected by their presidents to balance the ticket and appeal to a different constituency. Eight times in our history, the vice-president has become president following the death of the president. Each time, there was no provision to replace the vice-president until the next election. There was also no provision for a case of presidential incapacity. In 1967, the Twenty-fifth Amendment to the Constitution provided for replacing the vice-president and addressing presidential incapacity. The first use of the amendment occurred with the resignation of Nixon's vice-president, Spiro Agnew. Congress confirmed Gerald Ford as the new vice-president. When President Nixon resigned the next year, Gerald Ford, became the first non-elected president in our history. With congressional approval, President Ford selected Nelson Rockefeller as his vice-president [p. 445-447].

The Presidency: Issues for the New Century

The scope of the presidency has changed from chief clerk to world leader in the twentieth century. With the help of media, the president has become a "super star," and the image often obscures important policy issues. The task of regulating the economy and overseeing the government has become very difficult with the advent of "divided government." The role the president plays in engaging the nation in military action is another important issue that will remain in the new century [p. 448].

KEY TERMS

impeachment—p. 441

line-item veto—p. 430

National Security Council (NSC)—p. 445

Office of Management and Budget (OMB)—p. 444

Twenty-fifth Amendment—p. 447

White House Office—p. 444

CD-ROM *AMERICA AT ODDS*

SHOULD A SITTING PRESIDENT BE IMMUNE TO CIVIL LAWSUITS ? The interactive module for Chapter 13 presents the issue of civil lawsuits brought against the President. The module traces the history of lawsuit limits from the days of the Magna Carta in England. View the discussion about the role of public opinion in controlling abuses of power. You can use an interactive exercise to learn the facts about civil lawsuits, and make up your own mind about the issue. A ten-question interactive multiple-choice quiz reinforces key points in the material.

PRACTICE EXAM

(Answers appear at the end of this chapter.)

Fill-in-the-Blank. Supply the missing word(s) or term(s) to complete the sentence.

1. The _____ Amendment clarified aspects of Electoral College voting.

2. Decorating war heroes is an example of the president's role as chief _____ _____.

3.   The president is constitutionally bound to execute, or enforce, treaties, acts of Congress, and the

     judgements of federal courts in his role as _____ _____.

4.   Except in cases of impeachment, the constitution gives the president the power to grant _____

     and _____ for offenses against the United States.

5.   _____ _____ made between the president and other heads of state greatly

     enhance presidential power in foreign affairs

6.   Powers given to the president by law are called _____ _____.

7.   The formal indictment of the president by the House of Representatives is called _____.

8.   The presidential advisory group composed of the Secretaries of the executive departments is called the

     _____.

9.   The White House Office is coordinated by the _____ _____ _____.

10. The only duty of the vice-president found in the Constitution is to preside over the _____.

True/False. Circle the appropriate letter to indicate if the statement is true or false.
1.   T   F   A presidential candidate cannot win the Electoral College vote without getting a majority of
              the popular vote.
2.   T   F   In most democratic governments, the role of chief of state is given to someone other than the
              chief executive.
3.   T   F   The president's extensive appointment powers allow him to control and run the federal
              bureaucracy to suit his desires.

4. T F The president may grant reprieves and pardons for all offenses against the United States except in cases of contempt of court.

5. T F The president has the sole power to recognize or refuse to recognize foreign governments.

6. T F Executive agreements made by the president with the heads of other governments must be ratified by the Senate.

7. T F The presidential veto is an effective legislative tool because Congress rarely can override it.

8. T F Emergency powers are an example of inherent powers exercised by the president.

9. T F The president is required by law to spend all monies appropriated by Congress.

10. T F Most presidents have relied heavily on their cabinet members for advice in decision-making.

Multiple-Choice. Circle the correct response.

1. The most common occupation of presidents has been

    a. teachers.

    b. lawyers.

    c. businessmen.

    d. farmers.

2. In the event that no candidate receives a majority of Electoral College votes, the president is selected by the

    a. Senate from the two candidates receiving the highest electoral votes.

    b. Senate from any candidates receiving electoral votes.

    c. Congress from any person they choose to elect.

    d. House of Representatives choosing from the highest three candidates receiving electoral votes.

3. The activity most typical of the Chief of State role is

    a. developing military strategy.

    b. delivering the State of the Union Address.

    c. negotiating treaties with foreign governments.

    d. receiving visiting chiefs of state at the White House.

4. The president can remove all of the following from office except

    a. federal judges.

    b. the heads of cabinet departments.

    c. individuals within the Executive Office of the President.

    d. political appointees.

5. The Constitutional requirement that the president "shall be the Commander-in-Chief of the Army and Navy" is to

    a.   require the president to be a commissioned officer.

    b.   distort the lines of authority within the command structure of the armed forces.

    c.   require the president to take instruction at one of the service academies.

    d.   place the armed forces under civilian, rather than military, control.

6. The role in which the president has probably exercised more authority is

    a.   Chief Administrator.

    b.   Chief of his party.

    c.   Commander-in-Chief.

    d.   Chief Legislator.

7. The activity typical of the role of Chief Diplomat is

    a.   vetoing foreign policy legislation.

    b.   delivering the State of the Union Address.

    c.   meeting with state governors to discuss federal aid.

    d.   negotiating treaties with foreign governments.

8. A typical activity associated with the role of Chief Legislator is

    a.   recognizing representatives from foreign governments.

    b.   negotiating treaties with foreign governments.

    c.   meeting with state party leaders to discuss campaign strategy.

    d.   offering the annual State of the Union Address.

9. The only requirement of a president in issuing an executive order is that the executive order must

    a.   pertain to legislatively authorized items.

    b.   deal with only military matters.

    c.   deal only with the Executive Office of the President.

    d.   be published in the Federal Register.

10. Executive privilege

    a.   means that no member of the executive branch can be prosecuted for any act while performing his or her job.

    b.   is the concept that refers to the president's use of a pocket veto during a session of Congress.

    c.   protects the president and his cabinet from impeachment proceedings.

    d.   refers to the president's right to withhold certain information from congress and/or the courts.

11. The only president ever impeached by the House of Representatives was

a. Lyndon Johnson.

b. Andrew Johnson.

c. Richard Nixon.

d. Bill Clinton.

12. The agency that includes most of the key personal and political advisers to the president is in the

a. Cabinet.

b. Congress.

c. White House Office.

d. National Security Council.

13. Which statement is correct concerning the vice-president's job?

a. The Constitution gives several important powers to the vice-president.

b. The Constitution makes the vice-president the number one advisor to the president.

c. Earlier vice presidents had more to do than our recent vice-president did.

d. The constitution does not give much power to the vice-president.

14. The Constitutional amendment setting procedures for presidential succession and disability is the

a. Twelfth Amendment

b. Twenty-Fourth Amendment

c. Twenty-Fifth Amendment

d. Twenty-Seventh Amendment

15. The question of who shall be president if both the president and vice-president die is answered by the

a. Twenty-Fifth Amendment

b. Special election to fill the vacancy

c. Succession Act of 1947

d. Twelfth Amendment

Short Essay Questions. Briefly address the major concepts raised by the following questions.

1. Identify and explain the roles of the president.

2. Trace the development of the sources of presidential power.

3. Describe the organization of the executive branch, and how it has evolved over time.

4. Discuss the evolving role for the vice president as an advisor and successor to the president.

ANSWERS TO THE PRACTICE EXAM

Fill-in-the-Blank.

1. Twelfth [p. 420]
2. of state [p. 421]
3. chief executive [p. 422]
4. reprieves, pardons [p. 423]
5. executive, agreements [p. 427]

6. statutory powers [p. 433]
7. impeachment [p. 441]
8. cabinet [p. 442]
9. chief of staff [p. 444]
10. senate [p. 445]

True/False.

1. F [p. 420]	3. F [p. 422]	5. T [p. 426]	7. T [p. 432]	9. F [p. 441]
2. T [p. 421]	4. F [p. 423]	6. F [p. 427]	8. T [p. 433]	10. F [p. 443]

Multiple-Choice.

1. b [p. 419]	4. a [p. 422]	7. d [p. 426]	10. d [p. 439]	13. d [p. 445]
2. d [p. 420]	5. d [p. 423]	8. d [p. 428]	11. b [p. 442]	14. c [p. 447]
3. d [p. 421]	6. c [p. 425]	9. d [p. 439]	12. c [p. 444]	15. c [p. 448]

Short Essay Answers.

1. Identify and explain the roles of the president [p. 420-433].

    There are five constitutional roles of the president. These are (1) chief of state, (2) chief executive, (3) commander-in-chief, (4) chief diplomat, and (5) chief legislator.

    *   The chief of state role describes ceremonial functions such as decorating war heroes, hosting visiting chiefs of state, telephoning sports and space heroes, and dedicating parks.
    *   The chief executive role is to execute the laws. The president makes appointments of key individuals to carry out this function. He can also grant a reprieve and a pardon under executive authority.
    *   Commander-in-chief reflects the concept of civilian control of the military. This is probably the president's most powerful role.
    *   The chief diplomat role involves the making of treaties with the consent of the Senate, and recognizing foreign governments as legitimate.
    *   The chief legislator role includes the State of the Union message every year and the use of veto power over laws passed by Congress.

2.   Trace the development of the sources of presidential power [p. 433, 438-441].

There are four major sources of presidential power. These sources are (1) the Constitution, (2) statutes, (3) expressed power, and (4) inherent power.

*   Constitutional powers of the president are contained in Article II and are the powers discussed in essay one.

*   Statutory power is created for the president through laws enacted by Congress, such the power to declare national emergencies.

*   Expressed powers are those that are specifically written into the Constitution or laws.

*   Inherent powers are those that can be inferred from loosely worded constitutional statements, such as "executive power shall be vested in a President." Emergency powers invoked by the president during wartime are good examples of inherent powers.

3.   Describe the organization of the executive branch, and how it has evolved over time [p. 442-445].

*   The administration of George Washington created an advisory group, the cabinet, which was made up of the heads, or Secretaries, of the executive departments.

*   Beginning with President Andrew Jackson, presidents used an informal group of advisors called the kitchen cabinet.

*   President Franklin Roosevelt greatly expanded the administrative staff of the president by the creation of an Executive Office of the President (EOP) in 1939. The key parts of the EOP are

    ◊   the White House Office, which is coordinated by the chief of staff, and provides the president with what ever he needs to carry out his duties.

    ◊   the Council of Economic Advisers (CEA) advises the president on economic policy.

    ◊   the Office of Management and Budget (OMB) prepares the budget and advises the president on management and planning.

    ◊   the National Security Council advises the president on military and security issues.

4.   Discuss the evolving role for the vice-president as advisor and successor to the president [p. 445-448].

*   The only role for the vice-president stated in the Constitution is to preside over the Senate.

*   Vice-Presidents have traditionally been selected to balance the ticket.

*   Eight vice presidents have become presidents following the death of a president.

*   The Constitution provided no process to select a new vice-president.

*   The Twenty-fifth Amendment sets procedure for presidential succession and disability.

*   The Succession Act of 1947 provides for the situation in which both the president and vice-president die.

Chapter 14
The Bureaucracy

CHAPTER SUMMARY

The Nature of Bureaucracy

Bureaucracy is defined as a large organization that is structured hierarchically to carry out specific functions. Bureaucracies can exist in both the public and private sectors [p. 455]. Public bureaucracies do not have a single set of leaders, are not organized to make a profit, and are neither necessarily efficient nor respond quickly to change. Bureaucracies in the United States enjoy a greater degree of autonomy than bureaucracies in most other countries. The lack of government control of industry in the U.S. does not mean that administrative agencies do not regulate private industry [p. 457].

Theories of Bureaucracy

There are several different theories about how bureaucracies function.

- In the Weberian model, bureaucracies are rational, hierarchical organizations in which power flows from the top down [p. 457].
- In the Acquisitive model, top-level bureaucrats always try to expand their budget and staff.
- In the Monopolistic model, bureaucracies are like monopolies in that they are less efficient and more costly to operate.
- And in the Garbage Can model, a bureaucracy bumbles along aimlessly in search of solutions to particular problems [p. 458].

The Size of the Bureaucracy

The federal bureaucracy began with three departments, State, War, and Treasury, and a handful of employees; the office of Attorney General was added in 1789. Today, the fourteen executive departments of government, and other agencies, employ approximately 2.7 million employees. See Figure 14-1, page 459, for a look at government civilian employees by agency.

The Organization of the Federal Bureaucracy

The federal bureaucracy has four organinzational structures:

- cabinet departments

  The fourteen cabinet departments, described as line organizations, form the major part of the federal bureaucracy. See Table 14-2, page 464, for the year created, and brief description of each cabinet department.

- independent executive agencies

  Independent executive agencies are bureaucratic organizations that are not part of an executive department, but still report directly to the president. See Table 14-3, page 465 for the year created, and brief description of each agency.

- independent regulatory agencies

Independent regulatory agencies are responsible for supervising a particular sector of the economy in the public interest. The first agency established was the Interstate Commerce Commission (ICC) in 1887. See Table 14-4, page 466, for the year created, and brief description of each agency.

- government corporations.

  Government corporations are agencies that administer a quasi-business enterprise. The U.S. Postal Service is a good example of this type of bureaucratic structure. See Table 14-5, page 467, for the list, year created, and brief description of each government corporation.

Staffing the Bureaucracy

There are two categories of bureaucrat, political appointees and civil servants.

- Political appointees are appointed to the top positions in the government by the president. The average term of a political appointee is two years.

- The career civil servants, which make up the bulk of the bureaucracy, can afford to wait out political appointees with whom they disagree [p.467-468].

The federal civil service began in 1789 with a so-called natural aristocracy of society's "best citizens." When Andrew Jackson became president, he implemented a "spoils system" by awarding government jobs to his political supporters. In 1883, the Civil Service Reform Act, or Pendleton Act, replaced the spoils system with a merit system [p. 469] and created a Civil Service Commission to administer the personnel service. In 1939, the Hatch Act was passed to protect government workers from political manipulation [p. 470]. Finally, the Civil Service Reform Act of 1978 created the Office of Personnel Management (OPM), and the Merit Systems Protection Board (MSPB) [p. 471].

Modern Attempts at Bureaucratic Reform

The government continues to reform the bureaucracy and make it more responsive to U.S. citizens. In 1976, congress passed the Government in the Sunshine Act. This law required all multiheaded federal agencies to conduct their business regularly in public session [p. 471]. Sunset legislation, passed by most state legislatures but not by Congress, is designed to remove agencies on a regular basis, unless they are recreated with legislative action. Another approach to bureaucratic reform is contracting out services to the more efficient private sector. The Government Performance and Results Act of 1997 was designed to improve efficiency in the federal work force. Agencies were to set goals and establish a means of measuring if the goals were reached. The Merit Systems Protection Board (MSPB) created in 1978 was designed in part to protect whistleblowers who report bureaucratic waste and inappropriate behavior [p. 472-473].

Bureaucrats as Politicians and Policymakers

Congress is unable to oversee the day-to-day administration of its programs. Congress delegates this authority to administrative agencies through what is called enabling legislation. Rulemaking by these agencies does not take place in vacuum, but occurs in the public arena because new regulations must

141

be published in the Federal Register. Groups falling under regulation can engage in a process called negotiated rule-making. This process allows individuals and groups to participate in the final rule-making. Theories of bureaucracy once assumed that bureaucrats do not make policy decisions, but merely enforce these decisions. The concepts of iron triangle and issue networks hold that bureaucrats do play a major role in policy decisions [p. 474-477].

Congressional Control of the Bureaucracy

Although Congress cannot oversee the day-to-day operations of the bureaucracy, it can still control the bureaucracy by authorization and appropriation of funds, and by investigation and oversight hearings [p. 478].

The Bureaucracy: Issues for the New Century

Attempts to reform bureaucracy will continue in the new century. Competition in the private marketplace will continue to influence government bureaucracy. The actual job of the federal bureaucracy will never disappear as long as government exists, and reforms will be needed on a continual basis to make the bureaucracy accountable to the citizens.

KEY TERMS

acquisitive model—p. 458.

bureaucracy—p. 455.

Civil Service Commission—p. 470.

garbage can model—p. 458.

government corporation—p. 466.

Government In The Sunshine Act—p. 471

Hatch Act—p. 471.

CD-ROM *AMERICA AT ODDS*

BUREAUCRACY AND BIG GOVERNMENT. The interactive module for Chapter 14 reviews the characteristics of the classic or Weberian model of bureaucracy. See pro and con arguments for bureaucracy by President Clinton, and Senator Charles Grassley. You can use an interactive exercise to learn a few of the ways to reform the bureaucracy, and make it more responsive to the public. A ten-question interactive multiple-choice quiz reinforces key points in the material.

PRACTICE EXAM

(Answers appear at the end of this chapter.)

Fill-in-the-Blank. Supply the missing word(s) or term to complete the sentence.

1.   A _____ is a large organization which is structured hierarchically

and carries out specific functions.

2. The classic model of the modern bureaucracy is the _____ model.

3. The major service organizations of the federal government are the fourteen _____.

4. _____ _____ _____ are bureaucratic organizations that are

    not located within a department and report directly to the president.

5. The earliest independent regulatory agency to be created was the _____.

6. The newest form of a bureaucracy in the United States is the _____ _____.

7. The president who is associated with the spoils system is _____ _____.

8. Replacing government services with services from the private sector is called _____ _____.

9. The three-way alliance among legislators, bureaucrats, and interest-groups to benefit their respective

    interests is called the _____ _____.

10. The law that specifies the name, purpose, functions, and powers of an agency is _____.

True/False. Circle the appropriate letter to indicate if the statement is true or false.

1. T   F   Modern presidents have exerted power over and shaped the bureaucracy to their own policies.
2. T   F   The federal bureaucracy in the United States is much more controlled and restricted than in other countries.
3. T   F   Cabinet departments can be described in management terms as line organizations.

4. T   F   Regulatory agencies are independent because they are administered independently of all three branches of government.

5. T   F   The assassination of President James Garfield triggered civil service reform.

6. T   F   The Hatch Act prohibits federal civil service employees from engaging in political campaigns.

7. T   F   Today, few states have Sunset laws.

8. T   F   Contracting out government services is a reform that has been most successful at the local level of government.

9. T   F   Today, agencies and departments of government do not play an important role in policy-making because of tight control by Congress.

10. T   F   Congress can call on the General Accounting Office to investigate bureaucratic agencies.

Multiple-Choice. Circle the correct response.

1.   A basic distinction between private corporations and public bureaucracies is that private corporations

     a   have managers and public bureaucracies do not.

     b.   are organized to make a profit and public bureaucracies are not.

     c.   are efficient and public bureaucracies are not.

     d.   are generally large, complex enterprises, and Congress keeps public bureaucracies small.

2.   The view that top-level bureaucrats will always try to expand the size of budgets is the theory of the

     a   Weberian Model.

     b.   Acquisitive Model.

     c.   Monopolistic Model.

     d.   Garage Can Model.

3.   The image of the bureaucracy as a bumbling, rudderless organization is central to the

     a   Garbage Can Model.

     b.   Acquisitive Model.

     c.   Monopolistic Model.

     d.   Weberian Model.

4.   Since 1970, most of the growth in government employment has occurred at the

     a   municipal level.

     b.   state and local level.

     c.   national level.

     d.   county level.

145

5. The two groups of people in government who may call themselves bureaucrats are

    a.   members of Congress and their appointees.

    b.   the president and cabinet.

    c.   political appointees and civil servants.

    d.   state employees and members of Congress.

6. Thomas Jefferson brought into public service the so-called "natural aristocracy," which refers to

    a.   a cadre of permanent civil servants.

    b.   permanent patronage appointments.

    c.   a small ruling clique whose membership is based on birth, wealth, and ability.

    d.   loyal servants.

7. The Civil Service Reform Act (Pendleton Act) had the effect of

    a.   establishing in law the spoils system for political appointment.

    b.   establishing the principle of employment on the basis of open competitive exams.

    c.   preventing the best qualified people from being employed by the government.

    d.   allowing corruption and graft to enter the employment practices of government.

8. The idea of Sunset legislation was first suggested by President

    a.   Franklin Roosevelt.

    b.   Jimmy Carter.

    c.   Abraham Lincoln.

    d.   Ronald Reagan.

9. The major requirement imposed by the Government in the Sunshine Act is that

    a.   federal agencies and commissions have open meetings.

    b.   information about individuals and companies be made public.

    c.   secret meetings take place within the government.

    d.   all multi-headed federal agencies conduct their business regularly in public session.

10. The term Sunset legislation refers to

    a.   the idea that Congress must reauthorize programs annually.

    b.   legislation that protects a program so that the sun will never set on the program.

    c.   automatic program termination after a prescribed period unless Congress reauthorizes it.

    d.   built-in protections for program continuation.

11. Congress created agencies within the federal bureaucracy to

    a.   review proposed legislation.

    b.   implement legislation passed by Congress.

    c.   act as a sounding board for new laws.

    d.   control the actions of the president.

12. The "iron triangle" refers to

   a.   a policy of controlling information through censorship.

   b.   an alliance of mutual benefit among an agency, its client group, and congressional committees.

   c.   the mathematical formula used by the bureaucracy to determine benefit payments.

   d.   an alliance among Congress, the president, and big business to control the economy.

13. The ultimate check that Congress has over the bureaucracy is the ability to

   a.   hire and fire members of boards and commissions.

   b.   write legislation in specific terms so that the bureaucracy will not be able to interpret the meaning of laws.

   c.   withhold the appropriations of money to the bureaucracy.

   d.   influence the president to take action against a bureaucrat.

14. Negotiated rulemaking involves federal agencies in negotiations with

   a.   Congress.

   b.   the president.

   c.   the courts.

   d.   parties to be affected by a new rule.

15. Issue networks are

   a.   another name for "iron triangles."

   b.   a concept that illustrates how experts support issues or a particular policy position.

   c.   an attempt by the media to manipulate public opinion on a particular issue.

   d.   insider relationships within Congress to protect congressional benefits.

Short Essay Questions. Briefly address the major concepts raised by the following questions.

1. Identify and explain several theories of bureaucracy.

2. Discuss the different types of government agencies and organizations in the federal bureaucracy.

3. Describe the recent reforms in the federal civil service.

4. Explain the iron triangle and issue network models of the bureaucracy.

ANSWERS TO THE PRACTICE EXAM

Fill-in-the-Blank.

1. bureaucracy [p. 455]

2. Weberian [p. 457]

3. cabinet departments [p. 460]

4. Independent executive agencies [p. 462]

5. Interstate Commerce Commission [p. 463]

6. government corporation [p. 466]

7. Andrew Jackson [p. 469]

8. contracting out [p. 472]

9. iron triangle [p. 476]

10. enabling legislation [p. 474]

True/False.

1. F [p. 455]	3. T [p. 460]	5. T [p. 469]	7. F [p. 472]	9. F [p. 474]
2. F [p. 456]	4. T [p. 465]	6. T [p. 471]	8. T [p. 472]	10. T [p. 478]

Multiple-Choice.

1. b [p. 456]	4. b [p. 459]	7. b [p. 469]	10. c [p. 471]	13. c [p. 478]
2. b [p. 458]	5. c [p. 467]	8. a [p. 472]	11. b [p. 476]	14. d [p. 476]
3. a [p. 458]	6. c [p. 469]	9. d [p. 471]	12. b [p. 476]	15. b [p. 477]

Short Essay Answers

1. Identify and explain several theories of bureaucracy [p. 457-458].

    - There are four basic theories:
        ◊ The Weberian model
        ◊ The Acquisitive model
        ◊ The Monopolistic model
        ◊ The Garbage Can model.
    - The classic or Weberian model viewed bureaucracy as rational, hierarchical organization in which power flows from the top downward and decisions are based on logic and data.
    - The Acquisitive model focused on the concept that top level bureaucrats will want to maximize the size of their budgets and staff. The bureaucrat will try to ìsellî their public service to Congress and the public.
    - The Monopolistic model emphasized that bureaucracies are like monopolistic business firms, they have no competition. Monopolies tend to be less efficient and more costly to operate. This model arguing for the privatizing of some bureaucratic functions.
    - The Garbage Can model proposed that bureaucracy rarely acts in a coherent manner, but solves problems by costly trial and error methods.

2. Discuss the different types of government agencies and organizations in the federal bureaucracy [p. 459-467]. See Tables 14-2, page 464, 14-3, page 465, 14-4, page 466, and 14-5, page 467.

    - There are four major bureaucratic structures:
        ◊ cabinet departments
        ◊ independent executive agencies
        ◊ independent regulatory agencies
        ◊ government corporations.

- Cabinet departments are the fourteen executive departments, headed by a secretary, except for the Justice Department head by the Attorney General. These are the major service organizations of the national government.
- Independent executive agencies are federal agencies not part of a cabinet department but that report directly to the president. A good example is the Central Intelligence Agency. (CIA).
- Independent regulatory agencies are agencies administered independently of all three branches of government because they perform the functions of all three branches. A good example is the Federal Communication Commission (FCC) which regulates all communication by telegraph, cable, telephone, radio and television.
- Government corporations are government agencies that administer a quasi-business enterprise. A good example is the U.S. Postal Service, which at one time was a cabinet department.

3. Describe the recent reforms in the federal civil service [p. 471-474].

- The important actual and proposed recent reforms include sunshine laws, sunset laws, contracting out, efficiency incentives, and more protection for whistleblowers.
- Government in the Sunshine Act required all multi-headed federal agencies to hold public meetings.
- Sunset laws require agencies to be terminated automatically at the end of a designated period, unless specifically reauthorized. Congress has never implemented this law, but most states have passed sunset laws.
- Contracting out government services to private sector providers has been most successful at the local level for services like trash collection.
- The Government Performance and Results Act of 1997 was designed to encourage government agencies to set goals and create a system to measure their performance.
- In spite of the Whistle-Blower Protection Act of 1989, individuals who bring to public attention gross government inefficiency or illegal action, are not protected from losing their job.

4. Explain the iron triangle and issue network models of the bureaucracy [p. 476-477].

- The iron triangle is a way of describing the bureaucracy's role in the policy-making process. It consists of a three-way alliance among legislators in Congress, bureaucrats, and interest groups in a given policy area. Some examples are agricultural policy, weapon systems policy, and crime policy.
- The term issue networks is a more complex way to describe the bureaucracy's role in the policy making process. An issue network consists of individuals or groups of experts that support a particular policy position on a given issue. This includes scholars, media, and others not usually considered part of the iron triangle.

Chapter 15
The Judiciary

CHAPTER SUMMARY

The Common Law Tradition

The concept of common law originated in England as judge-made law, that is a body of law that grew out of judicial decisions shaped by prevailing custom. This concept has influenced the American judicial system. The two main components of common law are precedent, which is a court ruling that will bear on subsequent legal decisions in similar cases, and *stare decisis*, which means to stand on decided cases [p. 485].

Sources of American Law

The major sources of American law are federal and state constitutions, statutes passed by legislative bodies, administrative law, and case law. Constitutions set forth the general organization, powers, and limits of government. The U.S. Constitution is the supreme law of the land. Statutes or ordinances passed by national, state, and local governments have increasingly become important as courts apply these concepts to the general framework of common law. Case law is the rules and principles announced in court decisions, usually appeals courts [p. 486-487].

The Federal Court System

The United States has a dual court system, made up of the federal court structure and the courts of the fifty states. The federal courts are the U. S. district courts, which are the trial courts, thirteen U.S. courts of appeals, and the U.S. Supreme Court. See Figure 15-1, page 488, for an overview of the federal court system. Figure 15-2, page 489, shows the boundaries of the U. S. courts of appeals. The only court created in the U.S. Constitution is the Supreme Court, and it is the supreme law of the land. The state courts created by state constitutions are also under the authority of the U.S. Supreme Court. There is a common process that is followed by both court systems. The two parties in a lawsuit are the plaintiff, who initiates the suit, and the defendant, against whom the suit is brought. In recent years, interest groups have become more important in lawsuits, because they litigate, that is, bring the case to trial. Interest groups can also influence the judicial process by *amicus curiae* briefs, which express a group's viewpoint on the case. Class-action suits are also brought by groups to benefit all citizens who are affected by the same situation [p. 490].

The Supreme Court at Work

The Supreme Court term is from October to June each year. The Court is not required to hear a particular case, but several factors affect its decision. These factors include a legal question on which separate lower courts have ruled differently, and pressure from the solicitor general of the U.S. to review a case. The solicitor general represents the government in cases before the Supreme Court, and is sometimes referred to as the "Tenth Justice." The Court will issue a *writ of certiorari*, if it decides to hear a case. It takes four justices to agree to hear a case. This is called the rule of four. The Court decides a case by a process that begins with oral arguments by the attorneys representing the two parties. The justices will meet in private conference to discuss the arguments and decide the case. The decision can be unanimous, which happens rarely, or a majority decision, or a concurring opinion, in which a justice wishes to emphasize a particular part of the decision, or a dissenting opinion, which is important because it can form the basis for the creation of a new majority or precedent in the future [p. 492-494].

The Selection of Federal Judges

All federal judges are appointed by the president with the advice and consent of the Senate for a life time term. The concept of senatorial courtesy allows a senator of the president's political party to exercise control over the federal judge vacancies in his or her state, particularly for the district court positions. Senatorial courtesy does not apply to Court of Appeals and Supreme Court appointments [p. 495]. The Supreme Court appointments are among the most important appointments that the president makes. See Table 15-1, page 496, for the background of Supreme Court justices. Ideology plays a major role in the selection process for federal judges. Most presidents select judges of their own political party and ideology for the federal courts. Clinton has selected more women and members of minority groups to federal judgeships than any president before him. Ideology can also influence the Senate confirmation process. Presidents Nixon, Reagan, and Bush saw their nominees for the Supreme Court either rejected in or subjected to volatile Senate confirmation hearings [p. 498].

The Policymaking Function of the Courts

The battles over judicial appointments reflect the growing importance of the judiciary in policymaking through the tool of judicial review. Judicial review was established by the Supreme Court's decision in *Marbury v. Madison* (1803). See a discussion of this case on page 499. Judges hold different views of the Court's role in policymaking. Judicial activism is a doctrine holding that the Supreme Court should take an active role in using its powers to check the other institutions of government when they exceed their authority. Judicial restraint rests on the principle that the Court should defer to the decisions made by the institutions elected by the people [p. 500-502]. The current court named for Chief Justice William Rehnquist, is a more conservative court than in the past. President Clinton's appointments to the court have brought about a more balanced court between liberal and conservative. See page 503 for the current court members and ideological breakdown. The extensive influence of the Court today has produced a public debate about the amount of power the court has. Some critics want to see the power of the Court reduced [p. 505].

What Checks Our Courts?

The executive, the legislature, the public, and the judiciary itself check the power of the courts. The executive branch carries out judicial rulings; the court does not have enforcement powers. The president also exercises control over the federal courts by his appointment of new judges. Congress must authorize funding to implement court decisions, and can pass new laws in response to court decisions, or begin the constitutional amendment process [p. 506]. Public opinion can limit the power of the court, since it has no enforcement powers; its authority is linked to its stature in the eyes of the public. Finally, the traditions of the court, including its refusal to hear political questions, which courts believe should be decided by the elected branches, offer protection to the public from excessive court power [p. 507-508].

The Judiciary: Issues for the New Century

The role of the Supreme Court to interpret the Constitution will continue to be important in the new century. Issues such as free speech and abortion seem to be resolved, but continue to come back to the courts. The Internet will present many challenges, as the court seeks to apply old concepts and principles to this new reality.

KEY TERMS

amicus curiae brief—p. 490

appellate court—p. 488

class-action suit—p. 490

common law—p. 485

concurring opinion—p. 494

dissenting opinion—p. 494

judicial activism—p. 501

judicial restraint—p. 502

majority opinion—p. 494

oral arguments—p. 494

precedent—p. 485

rule of four—p. 493

senatorial courtesy—p. 495

stare decisis—p. 485

unanimous opinion—p. 494

writ of certiorari—p. 493

CD-ROM *AMERICA AT ODDS*

DUE PROCESS. The interactive module for Chapter 15 looks at the due process of law provisions that must be interpreted by the Supreme Court. You can role-play being a Supreme Court justice faced with the case of a college student caught with marijuana. Review major court decisions, such as *Miranda v. Arizona, Gideon v. Wainwright, Mapp v. Ohio,* and *Brewer v. Willliams.* See pro and con arguments for how to interpret due process rights. You can use an interactive exercise to look at the recent changes in laws relating to due process. A ten-question interactive multiple-choice quiz reinforces key points in the material.

PRACTICE EXAM

(Answers appear at the end of this chapter.)

Fill-in-the-Blank. Supply the missing word(s) or term(s) to complete the sentence.

1. The body of judge-made law that developed from England and is still used today in the United States

    is called _____ _____.

2. The practice of deciding new cases with reference to former decisions is based upon the doctrine of

    _____ _____.

3. The United States' dual court system consists of both _____ courts and _____ courts.

4. The Supreme Court's decision to hear a case is determined by the rule ____ _____.

5. A _____ _____ suit filed by an individual seeks damages for "all persons similarly situated."

6. By _____ of _____ the Supreme Court orders a lower court to send it the record of a

    case for review.

7. A _____ opinion is an opinion written by a Supreme Court justice who agrees with the

    majority opinion but for different reasons.

8. Federal judges may be removed through _____, although such action is extremely rare.

9. Court decisions are translated into action by _____ _____.

10. Justices advocating the doctrine of _____ _____ believe the Supreme Court

should defer to decisions made by elected representatives.

True/False. Circle the appropriate letter to indicate if the statement is true or false.
1. T F Most of American law is based on the English legal system.
2. T F Article III of the Constitution gives the power of judicial review to the U.S. Supreme Court.
3. T F Federal court jurisdiction is less limited than state court jurisdiction because the federal
          government has jurisdiction over all the country.
4. T F Federal courts have authority to rule on all issues relating to state laws and federal matters.
5. T F Interest groups no longer use *amicus curiae* briefs to influence Supreme Court decisions.
6. T F Federal judges are either appointed or elected depending upon the jurisdiction of their court.
7. T F The nomination of Supreme Court justices belongs solely to the president.
8. T F Ideology no longer plays a very important role in a president's choice for the Supreme Court.
9. T F The makeup of the federal judiciary is typical of the American public.
10. T F The ideology of the Rehnquist court is more conservative with respect to states' rights.

Multiple-Choice. Circle the correct response.
1. *Stare decisis* is a doctrine
    a. enabling court decisions to vary from case to case.
    b. providing guidance to judges when common law does not apply.
    c. encouraging the following of precedent or previous court decisions.
    d. requiring hearings about complaints arising from regulations.
2. The level of trial courts in the federal judicial hierarchy is the
    a. District courts.
    b. Court of Appeals.
    c. Supreme court.
    d. state courts.
3. Appellate jurisdiction means the authority of a court to
    a. serve as a trial court.
    b. hear cases for the first time.
    c. review decisions from a lower court.
    d. establish grand juries.

4.   A *writ of certiorari* is defined as an order

    a.   compelling an official to carry out his responsibilities.

    b.   guaranteeing the right to a fair and impartial trial by jury.

    c.   preventing some action from being carried out.

    d.   to a lower court to send a case to the higher court for review.

5.   A *writ of certiorari* is issued by the Supreme Court only when

    a.   a majority of justices vote for such a request.

    b.   four justices vote for such a request.

    c.   a unanimous Court supports such a request.

    d.   the Solicitor General approves such a request.

6.   The official who represents the national government in the Supreme Court is the

    a.   Attorney General.

    b.   Solicitor General.

    c.   Vice-President.

    d.   Chief Justice.

7.   A Justice who accepts the majority decision, but not the reasons for it, may write his/her own

    a.   minority opinion.

    b.   majority opinion.

    c.   *amicus curiae* opinion.

    d.   concurring opinion.

8.   In terms of enforcement powers, the Supreme Court

    a.   has now acquired its own police force.

    b.   relies upon the good will of the public to see that its decisions are enforced.

    c.   must rely on other units of government to carry out its decisions.

    d.   does not make decisions that have to be enforced.

9.   Dissenting opinions in a Supreme Court decision are important because

    a.   they allow justices to make symbolic statements.

    b.   they agree with the majority opinion, but for different reasons.

    c.   they often form the basis for arguments that reverse decisions and establish new precedent.

    d.   they allow opposition groups to express their opinions before the court.

10.   Senatorial courtesy is a concept that

    a.   allows the president to pick his choice for judge

    b.   can veto a presidents choice for judge

    c.   applies only to Supreme Court nominations

    d.   applies only to state court nominations

11. The courts that have become "stepping-stones" to appointment to the Supreme Court are the

    a   District Courts.

    b. State Supreme Courts.

    c. Courts of Appeals.

    d. Tax Court.

12. In terms of judicial philosophy, Chief Justice William Rehnquist is know as a

    a   liberal justice.

    b. swing vote.

    c. conservative justice.

    d. moderate pragmatist.

13. The justices who believe that the Court should use its power to alter or challenge the policy direction of Congress, state legislatures, or administrative agencies are advocating

    a   judicial restraint.

    b. judicial activism.

    c. strict constructionism.

    d. moderate pragmatism.

14. The tradition of the Court has led justices to refuse to hear cases which are

    a   justiciable disputes.

    b. political questions.

    c. between citizens of different states.

    d. a real controversy.

15. The appointments of President Clinton to the Supreme Court have elevated the number of

    a   women to record numbers.

    b. Democrats to record numbers.

    c. minority members to record numbers.

    d. liberal members to record numbers.

Short Essay Questions. Briefly address the major concepts raised by the following questions.

1. Identify and explain the common law tradition and other major sources of American law.

2. Discuss the process the Supreme Court uses to decide cases.

3. Describe the presidential appointment process for federal judges.

4. Explain the checks or limitations on the power of the federal courts.

ANSWERS TO THE PRACTICE EXAM

Fill-in-the-Blank.

1. common law [p. 485]
2. *stare decisis* [p. 485]
3. state, federal [p. 487]
4. of four [p. 493]
5. class-action [p. 490]

6. *writ of certiorari* [p. 493]
7. concurring [p. 494]
8. impeachment [p. 495]
9. judicial implementation [p. 506]
10. judicial restraint [p. 502]

True/False

1. F [p. 455]
2. F [p. 456]
3. T [p. 460]
4. T [p. 465]
5. T [p. 469]
6. T [p. 471]
7. F [p. 472]
8. T [p. 472]
9. F [p. 474]
10. T [p. 478]

Multiple Choice.

1. c [p. 485]
2. a [p. 488]
3. c [p. 489]
4. d [p. 493]
5. b [p. 493]
6. b [p. 493]
7. d [p. 494]
8. c [p. 504]
9. c [p. 494]
10. b [p. 495]
11. c [p. 496]
12. c [p. 502]
13. b [p. 501]
14. b [p. 508]
15. a [p. 498]

Short Essay Answers

1. Identify and explain the common law tradition and other major sources of American law [p. 485-487].
    *   Common law is a body of judge-made law that originated in England from decisions shaped according to prevailing custom.
    *   The other major sources of American law are federal and state constitutions, statutes, administrative law, and case law.
    *   Constitutions set forth the general organization, powers, and limits of government.
    *   Statutes are laws enacted by any legislative body at federal, state, or local level.
    *   Rules and regulation issued by administration agencies are a source of law.
    *   Case law includes judicial interpretations of all of the above sources of law.

2. Discuss the process the Supreme Court uses to decide cases [p. 492-495].
    *   The Supreme Court term begins in October and adjourns usually in June.
    *   The first important decision for the Court is to decide which cases to hear.
    *   Important factors to consider are whether a legal issue has been decided differently by two separate courts, and if the Solicitor General is pushing the case.
    *   If the Court decides to hear a case, four justices (Rule of four) must agree to issue a *writ of certiorari*.

- Oral arguments will be scheduled before the Court when attorneys representing each side will present their cases.
- A private conference will be held in which the justices discuss the case and decide on an opinion.
- Opinions can be unanimous, majority, concurring, and dissenting.

3. Describe the presidential appointment process for federal judges [p. 495-498].

- All federal judges are appointed by the president with Senate advice and consent for life-time terms.
- The first step in the process is nomination by the president.
- Senatorial courtesy can be a big factor in the nomination of federal district judges. A senator of the president's party has a great deal of influence over federal district judge appointments from the senator's state. Senators have less influence over appeals court nominees, and no influence on Supreme Court appointment.
- Ideology and political party background are two of the most important factors determining who is nominated for federal judgeships.
- The confirmation hearings in the Senate have been rather difficult in recent years with Presidents Nixon's and Reagan's Supreme Court nominees rejected by the Senate.
- President Bush's nomination of Clarence Thomas produced a volatile confirmation hearing in 1991, although Thomas was confirmed.

4. Explain the checks or limitations on the power of the federal courts [p. 506-508].

- Our judicial system is probably the most independent in the world, but there are important checks on the power of the courts. These checks are the executive, the legislature, the public, and the judiciary itself.
- The executive branch has the power of judicial implementation. The way in which court decisions are translated into action is solely the responsibility of the executive branch.
- Court rulings can be modified or overturned by lack of appropriations to carry out rulings, or
- Overturned by constitutional amendments.
- Public opinion is an important factor, since the Court has no enforcement powers; its authority is linked to its stature in the eyes of the public.
- Federal judges typically exercise self-restraint in making their decisions. Political questions are issues that a court defers to the decision-making of the executive or legislative branches.

Chapter 16
Domestic Policy

CHAPTER SUMMARY

The Policymaking Process

The beginning of the policymaking process is the recognition that a problem exists and needs a solution. The Personal Responsibility and Work Opportunity Reconciliation (Welfare Reform Act) of 1996 provides a good example of the creation of a policy. There are five basic steps in policymaking:

- agenda building

  Debate started in the 1930s when the major welfare programs began. Media coverage in the 1980s and 1990s put the welfare reform issue on the agenda.

- agenda formulation

  Compromise helped formulate the policy as welfare benefits were continued for two years.

- agenda adoption

  Congress passed the Welfare Reform Act of 1996.

- agenda implementation

  The major provisions of the law called for two more years of benefits, unless a recipient is working, lifetime benefits of five years total, more power to states to determine program guidelines, and provisions to deny benefits to unmarried teenage mothers.

- agenda evaluation [p. 519].

  Evaluation continues. Supporters of the reform point to a 27 percent nationwide drop in the number of people on welfare. Critics of the policy believe that the provision denying welfare assistance to unwed teenage mothers will only hurt poor children [p. 521].

While these steps are well understood, there are competing models of how and for whose benefit that process work. See Table 16-1, page 520, for a list and brief explanation of these models.

Poverty and Welfare

Historically, poverty has been accepted as inevitable. Industrialized wealthy nations like the United States have been able to eliminate mass poverty through income transfers. An array of welfare programs transfer income from wealthy to poor individuals. The official definition of poverty in the United States is $16,500 yearly income for an urban family of four. The poverty level varies with family size and location. See Figure 16-1, page 523, for a look at the official poverty numbers since 1959. In-kind subsidies, such as food stamps, low-income housing, and medical care are not usually counted as income. If these benefits are counted as income, the poverty rate drops. See Figure 16-2, page 524, for a look at different interpretations of poverty levels. In the wake of the Welfare Reform Act of 1996, the U.S. government provides the following low-income assistance: Temporary Assistance to Needy

Families (TANF), Supplemental Security Income (SSI), food stamps, and the earned-income tax credit (EITC) program [p. 523-524].

The Welfare Reform Act of 1996 gave states more control over welfare programs, but at the same time created major new problems for states to solve. The provisions of the law conflict with many state constitution mandates to take care of the needy, and require more enforcement provisions that states must pay for. The long-term effects of a loss of income to children in poor families may cause severe problems in the future. Finally, the loss of income may add to the problem of homelessness in the United States [p. 525-527].

Immigration

Immigration, like welfare, has been an issue of political debate that has lead to recent reform legislation. The upsurge in immigration rates in the past two decades has led to the fear that immigration is at record all time highs. Figure 16-4, page 528, shows that the level of immigration is close to all time highs, but the percentage of the U.S. population that is foreign born is still much lower than the peak immigration period of 1900-1910. The Immigration Reform Act of 1996 was designed to curb the flow of immigration, particularly illegal immigration. The act prohibited public assistance even to legal immigrants. This provision was later modified in response to criticism and concerns that this provision could violate the fourteenth amendment [p. 529-530].

Crime in the Twenty-first Century

Crime has been a major policy concern since the time of the American Revolution. Two crime issues that have been particularly significant are the rise in violent crimes and the increasing number of serious crimes committed by juveniles. See Figure 16-5, page 532, for a look at the violent crime rate in the United States from 1970 to the present time. The economic impact of crime in American society is massive. See Table 16-2, page 534, for an estimate of the costs. One of the major costs is building new jails and prisons. The United States now has the highest incarceration rates in the world. See page 535 for a comparison. Illegal drugs are recognized as a major source of crime. Two frequently mentioned methods of solving the drug problem are the get-tough policy of involving major new resources, such as the military, and the legalizing of drugs to take away the economic incentive. A third alternative is to allow states to experiment with these two different approaches [p. 535-536]. The fall in the crime rate since 1994 suggests that some policies on crime have worked. Some argue that the vast numbers of people in prison have reduced crime, while others believe that a relatively good economy reduces crime [p. 537].

Environmental Policy

The impact of human action on the environment has been a concern in the twentieth century with industrialization and population increases. Federal legislation began in the 1960s to protect the environment. See Table 16-3, page 539 for a list of major federal environmental legislation. The first major environmental legislation, caused by the Santa Barbara oil spill in 1969, was the National Environmental Policy Act. This act provided for an environmental impact statement (EIS) of major federal actions that might affect the quality of the environment [p. 538]. The Clean Air Act of 1990 addressed the air pollution caused by acid rain [p. 539]. The economic costs have become a significant political issue in the past two decades. The Superfund to clean up hazardous waste disposal sites has spent over $11 billion to clean up less than 10% of its high-priority sites [p.541].

Domestic Policy: Issues for the New Century

The issues of welfare reform and immigration have been linked in policy debate, as many legal and illegal immigrants receive benefits. Crime and balancing economic growth with the protection of the environment will continue to be important issues well into the next century [p. 541-542].

KEY TERMS

acid rain—p. 539

domestic policy—p. 517

earned-income tax credit (EITC)—p. 524

environmental impact statement (EIS)—p. 538

food stamps—p. 524

income transfer—p. 522

in-kind subsidy—p. 523

Supplemental Security Income (SSI)—p. 524

Temporary Assistance to Needy Families (TANF)—p. 523

CD-ROM *AMERICA AT ODDS*

WELFARE REFORM.   One interactive module for Chapter 16 looks at the issue of welfare reform. Explore some of the misperceptions that exist about welfare recipients, and benefits. Trace the history of benefits for the poor in U.S. history.   See the different views of the political parties on this issue. You can use an interactive exercise to look at the new provisions of the welfare reform act. A ten-question interactive multiple-choice quiz reinforces key points in the material.

STRICTER AIR QUALITY RULES. A second interactive module for Chapter 16 is on the issue of air quality standards. Learn about the major forms of air pollution. See the different views of the political parties on this issue. In an interactive exercise you can which pollutants are in the air in your part of the country.   A ten-question interactive multiple-choice quiz reinforces key points in the material.

PRACTICE EXAM

(Answers appear at the end of this chapter.)

Fill-in-the-Blank. Supply the missing word(s) or term(s) to complete the sentence.

1.   Courses of action on issues of national importance are called _____ _____.

2.   Selecting a specific strategy in the policymaking process is referred to as _____ _____.

3.   The Welfare Reform Act of 1996 shifted control of welfare to _____ government.

4.   Prior to 1965, United States immigration policy favored _____ _____.

5.   In the last few years the U. S. has had the _____ incarceration rate of any country in the world.

6. A disturbing element of crime in the U.S. is the number of serious crimes committed by _____.

7. The majority of arrests today in the U.S. are for crimes related to _____ _____.

8. The U.S. government has been addressing pollution since before the _____ _____.

9. The major environmental law prompted by the Santa Barbara oil spill was the _____

_____ _____ _____.

10. The purpose of the _____ is to regulate the clean-up of leaking hazardous

waste disposal sites.

True/False. Circle the appropriate letter to indicate if the statement is true or false.

1. T   F   The first step in the policymaking process is getting the issue on the agenda.
2. T   F   Historically throughout the world, poverty has been accepted as inevitable.
3. T   F   The poverty rate today is based on the consumer price index (CPI).
4. T   F   Measured as a portion of the population, immigration is more significant than in years past.
5. T   F   The Immigration Reform Act of 1996 doubled the number of border patrol agents.
6. T   F   Polls indicate that most Americans are worried about violent crime.
7. T   F   Violent crime has increased in the United States since 1994.
8. T   F   Only recently has the U.S. government begun to respond to the problems of pollution.
9. T   F   The United States is making fairly substantial strides in the war on toxic emissions.
10. T   F   90 percent of the Superfund money goes for the clean up of toxic waste sites.

Multiple-Choice. Circle the correct response.

1. The first step in solving a public problem is
   a. to determine the cost involved.
   b. to determine who will be helped and who will be harmed.
   c. for people to become aware of the problem.
   d. for the President to declare a state of emergency.

2. Public policymaking models differ from one another in identifying

   a. the variables associated with cost analysis.

   b. who the actors are in the process.

   c. the ease with which solutions can be accomplished.

   d. how and for whose benefit the process works.

3. A traditional solution to eliminate poverty has been

   a. work programs.

   b. payment vouchers.

   c. education training programs.

   d. transfer payments.

4. The United States has been able to eliminate mass poverty because of

   a. foreign aid from other countries.

   b. sustained economic growth.

   c. in increased work ethic.

   d. mass infusions of tax dollars.

5. The threshold income level for defining poverty was originally based on

   a. the consumer price index.

   b. the cost of a nutritionally adequate food plan by the U.S. Dept. of Agriculture.

   c. guidelines established by the Consumer Protection Agency.

   d. guidelines from the Farmers Union.

6. If the official poverty level were adjusted to include food stamps and housing vouchers it would

   a. significantly increase the number of people classified as living below the poverty line.

   b. dramatically lower the percentage of the population below the poverty line.

   c. only marginally lower the percentage of the population above the poverty line.

   d. effectively reduce the level of benefits.

7. The Welfare Reform bill of 1996 gave more control over welfare to

   a. the national government.

   b. state governments.

   c. local government.

   d. the private sector.

8. Performing public service jobs in return for welfare benefits is called

   a. workfare.

   b. jobfare.

   c. handouts.

   d. patronage.

9.   The fastest-growing subgroup of the homeless population is

   a.   street people.

   b.   the mentally ill.

   c.   illegal immigrants.

   d.   families.

10.   Prior to 1965, U.S. immigration policy favored

   a.   Asians.

   b.   White Europeans.

   c.   Native Americans.

   d.   Latin Americans.

11.   The Welfare Reform Act of 1996 originally prohibited public assistance to

   a.   all immigrants.

   b.   only illegal immigrants.

   c.   only illegal teenage immigrants.

   d.   only political refugees.

12.   From the mid-1980s to 1994 violent crimes committed by _____ significantly increased.

   a.   women

   b.   juveniles

   c.   immigrants

   d.   the elderly

13.   The majority of arrests today involve

   a.   murder.

   b.   drug offenses.

   c.   federal crimes.

   d.   white collar crimes.

14.   The main reason for continued overall air pollution from automobiles is

   a.   a lack of technology.

   b.   so many more automobiles being driven.

   c.   a lack of industry cooperation.

   d.   no laws regulate air pollution.

15.   The basic purpose of the Superfund is to

   a.   provide funding for election campaigns.

   b.   regulate the clean-up of leaking hazardous waste disposal sites.

   c.   fund basic research on causes of pollution.

   d.   provide operational expenses for the Environmental Protection Agency.

Short Essay Questions. Briefly address the major concepts raised by the following questions.

1.   Explain and discuss the steps in the policymaking process.

2.   Discuss the major provisions of the Welfare Reform Act of 1996. What impact will this act have on the poor in America?

3.   Analyze the issues of crime in the United States.

4.   Discuss the major laws attempting to protect the nation's environment.

ANSWERS TO THE PRACTICE EXAM

Fill-in-the-Blank.

1.   domestic policy [p. 517]   6.   juveniles [p. 532]

2.   agenda adoption [p. 519]   7.   drug offenses [p. 535]

3.   state [p. 520]   8.   American Revolution [p. 538]

4.   white Europeans [p. 529]   9.   National Environmental Policy Act [p. 538]

5.   highest [p. 535]   10. Superfund [p. 540]

True/False.

1.	T [p. 517]	3.	T [p. 523]	5.	T [p. 529]	7.	F [p. 532]	9.	T [p. 539]
2.	T [p. 522]	4.	F [p. 528]	6.	T [p. 531]	8.	F [p. 538]	10.	F [p. 541]

Multiple-Choice.

1.	c [p. 517]	4.	b [p. 522]	7.	b [p. 524]	10.	b [p. 529]	13.	b [p. 535]
2.	d [p. 519]	5.	b [p. 523]	8.	a [p. 526]	11.	a [p. 529]	14.	b [p. 539]
3.	d [p. 522]	6.	b [p. 523]	9.	d [p. 527]	12.	b [p. 532]	15.	b [p. 540]

Short Essay Answers

1.   Explain and discuss the steps in the policy-making process [p. 517-519].

   •   The policymaking process contains five major steps.

   •   Agenda building is the first step of recognition of a problem. The media, strong personalities, and interest groups usually facilitate this step.

   •   Agenda formulation is the discussion between the government and the public of various proposals to solve the problem. .

   •   Agenda adoption is the selection by Congress of a specific strategy from the proposals, which were discussed.

   •   Agenda implementation is the government action implemented by bureaucrats, the courts, police, and individual citizens.

- Agenda evaluation is groups inside and outside receiving "feedback" about the policy.

2. Discuss the major provisions of the Welfare Reform Act of 1996. What impact will this act have on the poor in America? [p. 519-522]

- The Welfare Reform Act shifted to state governments some of the financial burden of, and control over, the welfare system. The Aid to Families with Dependent Children (AFDC) program was abolished. A state-administered program funded by national government grants, called Temporary Assistance to Needy Families (TANF) was created to replace AFDC. The food-stamp program was retained by the national government, but the benefits were reduced.

- One of the basic aims of the act was to reduce welfare spending by all levels of government in the long run. To accomplish this, two major changes were made in the welfare system.

- One major change involved limiting most welfare recipients to two years of assistance, unless the recipient is working. Lifetime welfare assistance was limited to five years.

- The second major change was to deny benefits to unmarried teenage mothers.

- Supporters of the act point to a 27 percent decline in the number of people on welfare. It is difficult to say what percentage of this group has found jobs to replace welfare benefits.

- Critics of the act say that the new system makes it difficult for the truly needy to find assistance, and believe the provision to deny assistance to unwed teenage mothers will only hurt poor children.

3. Analyze the major issues of crime in the United States.

- Crime has been around since the days of the American Revolution.

- Two recent trends that concern Americans are violent crime and serious crimes committed by juveniles.

- Violent crime rose steadily from 1970 to 1986. See Figure 16-5, page 532.

- Juvenile crime rose dramatically from the mid-1980s to 1994. See Figure 16-6, page 533.

- Two major issues of crime in the United States are costs to society and the prison population.

- The yearly cost of crime is estimated at $450 billion. See Table 16-2, page 534.

- The United States has the highest incarceration rate of any country in the world.

- A major cause of crime in America is illegal drugs. Three alternative ways to address drug use have been proposed. These are a get-tough policy, legalization of all drugs, and letting states experiment with these two solutions.

4. Discuss the major laws attempting to protect the nation's environment [p. 538-541].

- Government legislation to control pollution can be traced back before the American Revolution. See Table 16-3, page 539 for major federal environmental legislation.

- The most concerted effort to clean up the environment begins in 1969 with the passage of the National Environmental Policy Act. This law provides for an environmental impact statement (EIS) to be prepared for all major federal actions that may impact the environment.
- The 1990 Clean Air Act was designed to clean up air pollution. A major environmental problem of air pollution was acid rain.
- In 1980, Congress passed the Superfund Act. This law provided money to clean-up leaking hazardous waste disposal site. In the late 1990s, less than 10 percent of the high-priority list sites had been cleaned up.
- The costs of cleaning up the environment have become a major political issue in the 1990s.

Chapter 17
Economic Policy

CHAPTER SUMMARY

The Politics of Taxes and Subsidies

Public policymaking is complicated, and nowhere is that more apparent than in economic policy where each policy action carries costs and benefits, known as policy trade-offs. In the world of taxes and subsidies, for every action on the part of government there is a reaction on the part of the affected public. This is known as the action-reaction syndrome [p. 549]. Individuals and corporations facing high taxes will have a big incentive to find or add loopholes to the tax laws. The 1986 attempt to simplify the tax code was undermined by adding new loopholes to the tax laws. This probably means that we will never have a simple tax code. Another way that people try to avoid paying taxes is to be involved in the underground economy. See Table 17-2, page 551, for estimates of the underground economy, and page 552 for a comparison of the underground economy in selected countries.

Social Security: How Long Will It Last?

The question of taxes in America always raises a discussion of the Social Security tax. The tax on employees and employers is a regressive tax in which people with higher incomes pay lower tax rates than people with lower incomes [p. 552]. The program is basically a pay-as-you-go transfer system in which those who are working pay benefits to those who are retired. The number of people working is declining relative to the number of people retiring, and the large numbers of the baby boom generation will bankrupt the current system when they retire beginning in the early twenty-first century. Numerous proposals to save the Social Security system have focused on allowing individuals to make private investments of social security taxes. No policy decision has been made, but a decision must be made, as nothing can be done to stop the aging of the population [p. 553-554].

The Politics of Fiscal and Monetary Policy

Changes in taxes are sometimes part of an overall fiscal policy change. A fiscal policy is the use of government spending or taxation to alter the national economy. One approach to fiscal policy is to use government funds to stimulate economic activity in a recession by increasing expenditures and decreasing taxes. Known as Keynesian economics, this policy grew out of the theories of the English economist John Maynard Keynes. Conversely, during inflation, the government should reduce spending and increase taxes to balance the economy [p. 555].

A monetary policy is also used to alter the economy by controlling the amount of money in circulation, which can affect interest rates, credit, inflation, and employment. Monetary policy works in a similar way to fiscal policy. In times of recession, the economy is stimulated by a greater supply of money and credit. With inflation, the money supply, and hence credit, is reduced to bring down the level of economic activity. The Federal Reserve System, called the Fed and created in 1913, largely carries out monetary policy. The chairperson of the system usually speaks for the entire board. The Fed and its Federal Open Market Committee (FOMC) make decisions about monetary policy eight times a year. Although monetary policy can be implemented much quicker than fiscal policy, it still seems to take over a year to affect the economy. In recent years, the Fed's record has been mixed at best, as some actions seem to have affected the economy in the wrong way [p. 556-558].

The Public Debt and the Disappearing Deficit

Until the late 1990s, the federal government had run a deficit in every year except two since 1960. A deficit results from spending more than revenues allow, and issuing U.S. treasury bonds to borrow the difference. The accumulation of all past deficits is known as the national debt [p. 559] or public debt and has been a major policy issue. While the government cannot go bankrupt as long as it makes interest payments, public debt financing by selling bonds can "crowd out" private borrowing and slow the rate of economic growth. Raising taxes finally eliminated the "permanent" federal budget deficit in the late 1990s. See Figure 17-3, page 562, for a look at higher taxes from 1957 to 1997. A new problem has recently emerged as politicians now face a budget surplus to spend.

Freer World Trade and the World Trade Organization

At the close of World War II, the United States was the most powerful economy in the world. This situation continued for twenty- five years. In the last few decades, Japan, the European Union, and other nations of the Pacific Rim have challenged U.S. dominance in the global marketplace. The current situation seems to be favorable to the United States even with a big deficit in balance of trade. The United States, as one of the world economic powers, can no longer take this position for granted [p. 562-563]. In general, the United States has been a leader in trying to ease restrictions on international trade. The reduction of tariffs was accomplished by the creation of the General Agreement on Tariffs and Trade (GATT) in 1947. In 1995, GATT was replaced by the World Trade Organization (WTO). The WTO has raised serious political issues, which must be resolved, if we are going to have a truly global economy [p. 566].

Economic Policy: Issues for the New Century

Social Security will continue to be a major issue in the next century as our population continues to age. The global economy will also continue to develop, and the issue of the U.S. economic role in the global economy will be a major economic policy decision.

KEY TERMS

action-reaction syndrome—p. 549

constant dollars—p. 559

the Federal Reserve

Federal Open Market Committee (FOMC)—p. 556

fiscal policy—p. 554

Keynesian economics—p. 555

loophole—p. 550

monetary policy—p. 554

public debt or national debt—p. 559

public debt financing—p. 560

regressive tax—p. 552

tariff——p. 566

underground economy—p. 551

U.S. Treasury Bond—p. 559

CD-ROM *AMERICA AT ODDS* [no module for Chapter 17]

PRACTICE EXAM

(Answers appear at the end of this chapter.)

Fill-in-the-Blank. Supply the missing word(s) or term to complete the sentence.

1. Individuals and corporations facing high taxes will always react by making concerted efforts to get

    Congress to insert _____ in new tax laws.

2. The _____ _____ refers to individuals who work for cash payments without

    paying any taxes.

3. The Social Security system is a pay-as-you-go transfer system in which those who are _____

    pay benefits to those who are _____.

4. Traditional fiscal policy _____ taxes during recessions and _____ them

    during times of inflation.

5. The economic theory associated with using fiscal policy to alter national economic variables is

    called _____ _____.

6. An economic condition with rising inflation and rising unemployment is defined as _____.

7. Federal Reserve monetary policy is made through the Federal _____ _____ _____.

8. When the federal government incurs a budget deficit, it issues debt instruments in the form of

    _____ _____ _____.

9. Foreigners own over 38 percent of the United States _____ _____.

10. With the formation of the _____ _____ in 1992, the U.S. slipped to second place

    in world economies.

True/False. Circle the appropriate letter to indicate if the statement is true or false.

1. T   F   The action-reaction syndrome was solved by the 1986 Tax Reform Act.

2. T   F   Because of recent reforms, the Social Security system will remain financially sound well into
              the twenty-first century.

3. T   F   Fiscal policy is primarily the responsibility of the president and Congress rather than the
              Federal Reserve Board.

4. T   F   The majority of adults today like the idea of directing part of their Social Security taxes to a
              personal retirement account in the private sector.

5. T   F   When the economy is in a recession, the Federal Reserve Board will usually increase the
              amount of money in circulation.

6. T   F   Monetary policy can be more quickly implemented than fiscal policy.

7. T   F   Members of the Federal Reserve Board are appointed for fourteen year terms.

8. T   F   Increased taxes eliminated the federal deficit in 1998.

9. T   F   One consequence of federal debt financing is that it tends to crowd out private borrowing.

10. T   F   The General Agreement on Tariffs and Trade (GATT) was replaced by the World Trade
              Organization (WTO) in 1995.

Multiple-Choice. Circle the correct response.

1. Legal methods in the tax code of avoiding taxes are referred to as

   a. justifications.

   b. hidden benefits.

   c. loopholes.

   d. give-backs.

2. The underground economy refers to

   a. all those goods and services produced underground.

   b. large corporations that are involved in mining operations.

   c. individuals who work for cash in order to avoid paying taxes.

   d. all service industries.

3. Under a regressive tax,

   a. people with high incomes pay a lower percentage in taxes than people with low incomes.

   b. you pay according to your ability.

   c. low income groups are treated fairly.

   d. the national debt is adversely affected.

4. Social Security taxes are

   a. based upon the Consumer Price Index.

   b. actually paid by the government.

   c. progressive taxes.

   d. regressive taxes.

5. Policies regulating the amount of money in circulation are part of a

   a. fiscal policy.

   b. national economizing.

   c. monetary policy.

   d. zero sum budgeting.

6. Regulating government spending or taxes to alter national economic variables is part of a

   a. stagflation.

   b. monetary policy.

   c. real assessed economic policy.

   d. fiscal policy.

7. A typical strategy for overcoming a recession would be to

    a.   decrease the supply of money in circulation.

    b.   increase the supply of money in circulation.

    c.   increase the tax base within the economy.

    d.   tax the underground economy to generate more revenue.

8. With rising inflation, the Federal Reserve will usually

    a.   cut back on the rate of growth of the money supply.

    b.   increase the rate of growth of the money supply.

    c.   relax interest rates.

    d.   instruct the president to reduce taxes.

9. Monetary policy does not suffer from the same lengthy time lags as fiscal policy does, because

    a.   monetary policy does not have an immediate effect upon consumers.

    b.   the president can act more quickly than congress to implement monetary policy.

    c.   the Federal Reserve can, within a very short time, put its policy into effect.

    d.   Congress can act quickly when needed to solve economic problems.

10. To pay for a budget deficit, the federal government

    a.   will usually sell off public land holdings.

    b.   will almost always increase taxes.

    c.   issues debt instruments in the form of U.S. Treasury bonds.

    d.   increases the amount of money in circulation.

11. Compared to the public debt of most European countries, the U.S. public debt is

    a.   larger than most.

    b.   comparatively low.

    c.   comparatively high.

    d.   difficult to measure because of U.S. accounting processes.

12. The U.S. economy has slipped to second place in world economies because of the

    a.   economic power of the Pacific Rim countries.

    b.   inefficiency of American workers.

    c.   establishment of the European Union.

    d.   labor union demand for higher wages.

13. The use of fiscal policy to alter economic variables is the underlying premise for

    a.   supply and demand.

    b.   Keynesian economics.

    c.   Marxist economic theory.

    d.   the global economy.

14. A tax on imported goods is

    a.   a tariff.

    b.   advocated by the World Trade Organization.

    c.   part of the European Union strategy.

    d.   necessary to pay for the global Internet.

15. A major concern about the World Trade Organization is that it will

    a.   strengthen multi-national corporation.

    b.   eliminate unionization of workers in developing nations.

    c.   increase tariffs on goods from non-member countries.

    d.   weaken environmental, health and safety laws.

Short Essay Questions. Briefly address the major concepts raised by the following questions.

1. Identify the difference between fiscal policy and monetary policy.

2. Discuss the action-reaction syndrome. How does it affect our federal tax system?

3. Identify the differences between the federal deficit and the national debt.

4. Explain the world trade position of the United States in the global economy of today

ANSWERS TO THE PRACTICE EXAM

Fill-in-the-Blank.

1. loopholes [p. 550]   6. stagflation [p. 556]

2. underground economy [p. 551]   7. Open Market Committee [p. 556]

3. working, retired [p. 553]   8. Treasury bonds [p. 559]

4. lowering, raising [p. 555]   9. public debt [p. 560]

5. Keynesian economics [p. 555]   10. European Union [p. 562]

True/False.

1. F [p. 549]	3. T [p. 554]	5. T [p. 556]	7. F [p. 558]	9. T [p. 560]
2. F [p. 553]	4. T [p. 553]	6. T [p. 557]	8. T [p. 562]	10. T [p. 566]

Multiple Choice.

1. c [p. 550]	4. d [p. 552]	7. b [p. 556]	10. c [p. 559]	13. b [p. 555]
2. c [p. 551]	5. c [p. 554]	8. a [p. 556]	11. b [p. 561]	14. a [p. 566]
3. a [p. 552]	6. d [p. 554]	9. c [p. 557]	12. c [p. 562]	15. d [p. 566]

Short Essay Answers

1. Discuss the action-reaction syndrome. How does it affect our federal tax system? [p. 549-551]

    *   The concept of the action-reaction syndrome is that for every action on the part of government, there is a reaction on the part of the affected public. The government attempts to counter the reaction with another action, which starts the cycle all over.

    *   This affects our tax system because individuals and corporation react by lobbying Congress to add loopholes to the tax laws. A loophole is a legal method to reduce the tax liabilities owed to the government. As more and more loopholes are added to the tax law, it becomes more and more complex.

    *   After years of criticism of the tax laws, the 1986 Tax Reform Act simplified the tax laws. We are now in the process of adding tax loopholes to the 1986 law.

2. Identify the difference between fiscal policy and monetary policy [p. 554-556].

    *   Fiscal policy is the change in government spending or taxation to alter national economic variables.

    *   Fiscal policy is under the control of Congress and the president.

    *   In a recession, which is a period of rising unemployment, the government will stimulate the economy by increasing government expenditures and by decreasing taxes. During inflation, which is rapid increases in employment and rising prices, the government will "cool off" the economy by reducing expenditures and increasing taxes.

    *   Monetary policy is the change in the amount of money in circulation to alter national economic variables.

    *   Monetary policy is under the control of the Federal Reserve System, or the Fed.

    *   In a recession, the Fed will stimulate the economy by expanding the rate of growth of the money supply. During inflation, the Fed will "cool offi"the economy by reducing the rate of growth of the amount of money in circulation.

3. Identify the differences between the federal deficit and the national debt. How does the government deal with national debt? [p. 559-562]

    *   The federal deficit occurs when the federal government spends more money in a year than it receives. From 1960 to 1998, the federal government usually operated at a deficit.

    *   The national debt is the total amount of debt carried by the federal government from all yearly deficits.

    *   Public debt financing is a process of issuing or selling U.S. Treasury bonds. The government can never go bankrupt, as long as it can make interest payments.

    *   Public debt financing can effect the economy by "crowding out" private borrowing.

    *   The federal deficit was ended in 1998 by the increase in taxes.

4. Explain the world trade position of the United States in the global economy of today [p. 562-566].

   - From the end of World War II to the 1960s, the United States was the most powerful economy in the world.

   - Over the last twenty-five years, the United States has been challenged by Japan, and other countries of the Pacific Rim. The creation of the European Union out of the fifteen countries of the former European Community created the worlds largest economy, aand the United States slipped into second place.

   - The United States faces a major problem of a deficit in its balance of trade, which reached record levels in 1998. Part of the balance of trade deficit, however, is because of the strength of the U.S. economy. Foreigners invest in our government and corporation bonds because of the U.S. economy.

   - The United States has been very active in supporting world trade through the lowering of tariffs with the General Agreement on Tariffs and Trade (GATT), and the World Trade Organization (WTO), which replaced GATT in 1995.

Chapter 18
Foreign and Defense Policy

CHAPTER SUMMARY

What is Foreign Policy?

> Foreign policy is a nation's external goals and the techniques and strategies used to achieve them. Two key aspects of foreign policy are national security, the protection of the independence and political integrity of the United States, and diplomacy, the settlement of disputes and conflicts among nations by peaceful methods [p. 573-574].

Morality versus Reality in Foreign Policy

> From the beginning of the United States, Americans have felt a special destiny to provide moral leadership to the rest of the world. Many of the U.S. foreign policy initiatives seem to be rooted in moral idealism. This philosophy sees all nations as willing to cooperate and agree on moral standards for conduct. The Peace Corps, established by President Kennedy, is a good example of this concept. In opposition to the moral perspective is political realism. This philosophy sees the world as a dangerous place in which each nation strives for survival. The United States has generally pursued a foreign policy that attempts to balance these philosophies [p. 574-575].

Who Makes Foreign Policy?

> While the President has important foreign policy powers, the Constitution gives Congress the opportunity to review these powers. The two most significant presidential powers are the negotiation of treaties and leadership of the armed forces as commander-in-chief. But Congress has the authority to declare war, and the Senate must ratify treaties by a two-thirds vote. Presidents have used executive agreements to get around the requirement of Senate-approved treaties. Finally, the Constitution gives the President the right to appoint ambassadors and recognize foreign governments.

> The President also has informal powers in the foreign policy process. These powers are his access to intelligence from the CIA and military, his ability to influence budget priorities, and his influence on public opinion [p. 575-576]. In addition to the president, there are at least four foreign policymaking sources within the executive branch. These are:
> - the Department of State, the executive agency most directly engaged in day-to-day foreign policy
> - the National Security Council, responsible for advising the president on domestic, foreign, and military policies affecting national security
> - the intelligence community, composed of all government agencies involved in intelligence activities. See page 578 for a list of the most important intelligence agencies.
> - the Department of Defense which brings all military agencies under one organization [p. 577-579].

Limiting the President's Power

The struggle between the president and Congress over foreign policy questions reached a highpoint during the Vietnam War (1964-1975). In 1973, Congress passed, over President Nixon's veto, the War Powers Resolution. This law required the president to "consult" with Congress before using troops in military action. Congress has also been more cautious in supporting the president where military involvement of American troops is possible. This has restored some of the balance of the relationship of the president and Congress in foreign policy [p. 579-580].

Domestic Sources of Foreign Policy

Besides the president and Congress, foreign policy is also influenced by sources in society, which include elite and mass opinion, and the military-industrial complex. Public opinion of the attentive public, that portion of the general public that pays attention to foreign policy issues, is particularly important. This segment represents about 10 to 20 per cent of all citizens. The military-industrial complex, which President Eisenhower warned the nation about, is the mutually beneficial relationship between the armed forces and defense contractors [p. 580-581].

The Major Foreign Policy Themes

An historical review of American foreign policy reveals several major themes. In the early days of our nation, the founding fathers held a basic mistrust of alliances with European nations. The Monroe doctrine of 1823 set forth a U.S. policy of isolationism toward Europe, a policy characterized by abstaining from an active role in international affairs or alliances, particularly with Europe. The end of the isolationist policy started with the Spanish-American War in 1898, and continued through World War I (1914-1918). This policy is generally called interventionism. After World War I, America returned to a policy of isolationism. World War II shattered isolationism forever, with the Japanese attack on Pearl Harbor, Hawaii on December 7, 1941. This event ushered in the period of internationalism in American foreign policy, which continues today [p. 583].

The United States and the Soviet Union were wartime allies against Adolph Hitler's Germany. After the war, the alliance fell apart, and the United States and the Soviet Union, in a Cold War, began a 50-year struggle for supremacy [p. 584]. The Soviet Union seized Eastern Europe and divided Europe by what Winston Churchill called an "iron curtain." The United States adopted a policy of containment by a series of encircling military alliances to prevent the spread of communist government. The military alliances were tested in a series of military actions, usually by "client" nations of each side. In the Korean War (1950-1953), and the Vietnam War (1964-1975), the United States engaged directly in military action [p. 585]. The Cuban Missile Crisis in 1962 brought the world to the brink of nuclear war, but after this crisis was peacefully negotiated, the United States, and the Soviet Union began a period of relaxed tension called détente. The Strategic Arms Limitation Treaty (SALT) began a process of reducing nuclear weapons [p. 586]. President Reagan's hard stand with the Soviet Union recalled the early days of the Cold War. Reagan's proposal for an expensive, space-based, missile defense system led to the collapse of the Soviet economy and the end of the Cold War [p. 587].

Challenges in World Politics

As the decade of the 1990s began, the Soviet Union, withdrawing from Eastern Europe, began economic and political changes that led to its collapse. A number of new republics were created including the largest part of the old Soviet Union, Russia. The dissolution of the Soviet Union brought a lowering of tensions among the nuclear powers, but the number and location of nuclear weapons continues to be a major problem. See Table 18-1, page 589, for a view of the number of nuclear weapons in the world.

In a new development, dissident groups, rebels, and other revolutionaries have used modern weapons to engage in terrorism in order to affect world politics. The long-standing regional conflict in the Middle East has produced a number of terrorist acts worldwide [p. 590]. The emergence of China, as a major trading partner of the United States and the most populous nation in the world, has altered world trade policies. This is just one of the major developments of the Global economy. Since the 1980s, the United States has become a debtor nation[p. 591-592]. We owe more to foreigners than foreigners owe to us.

Regional conflicts all over the globe have replaced the Cold War as a major focus of U.S. foreign policy. Unrest in the island nations of Haiti and Cuba produced a flood of immigration, which has particularly affected the state of Florida [p. 593-594]. Conflict in the Middle East, between Israel and its Arab neighbors, has been a concern of the United States since the conflict began in 1948. In a related mid-east issue, the United States sent more than a half-million troops to push Iraq out of Kuwait in 1991 [p. 594-596]. The collapse of the former Yugoslavia in Eastern Europe required the intervention of the United States and European nations to prevent the Serbs from killing ethnic groups. Ethnic violence in Africa has also flared in the 1990s. The United States has played little role in these conflicts, except for a limited effort to bring humanitarian aid to Somalia in 1992-1995 [p. 599].

Foreign and Defense Policy: Issues for the New Century

The end of the Cold War has altered the needs of the U.S. military to protect the security of the United States. Regional conflicts will continue to require a more flexible military force. The United States will need to cooperate with organizations like the United Nations to work with other nations to resolve conflicts. The global economy and global issues will become more important to the United States in the next century [p. 599].

KEY TERMS

attentive public—p. 581

cold war—p. 585

containment—p. 585

détente—p. 586

foreign policy—p. 573

intelligence community—p. 578

iron curtain—p. 585

isolationist foreign policy—p. 583

military-industrial complex—p. 581

Monroe Doctrine—p. 583

moral idealism—p. 574

National Security Council (NSC)—p. 573

political realism—p. 574

Strategic Arms Limitation Treaty (SALT I)—p. 586

CD-ROM *AMERICA AT ODDS*

THE U.S. AS WORLD POLICEPERSON. The interactive module for Chapter 18 looks at United States military intervention in the world. Explore how many times the United States has sent troops into other nations and see the views of the founding fathers on this issue. Look at the history of U.S. intervention by declared war and interventions without a declaration of war. You can use an interactive exercise to see recent viewpoints of the political parties. A ten-question interactive multiple-choice quiz reinforces key points in the material.

PRACTICE EXAM

(Answers appear at the end of this chapter.)

Fill-in-the-Blank. Supply the missing word(s) or term(s) to complete the sentence.

1.   _____ _____ describes U.S. goals, techniques, and strategies in the world arena.

2.   _____ refers to the peaceful settlement of disputes and conflicts among nations.

3.   The _____ _____ is the executive agency most directly engaged in foreign affairs.

4.   The _____ _____ formed the basis for the U. S. foreign policy of isolationism.

5.   The lasting change in American foreign policy came with the end of _____ _____ _____.

6.   The George F. Kennan doctrine, which became the bible of western foreign policy, was _____.

7.   President Eisenhower warned the nation about the influence of the _____ _____ _____.

8.   The French word that means a relaxation of tensions is _____.

9.   The United States currently imports more goods and services than it exports; it has a _____ _____.

10.   China sought and was granted _____ _____ _____ _____ for tariffs and trade by the U.S.

True/False. Circle the appropriate letter to indicate if the statement is true or false.

1.   T   F   National security policy covers the defense of the U.S. against actual or potential enemies.
2.   T   F   Diplomacy defines the techniques of negotiation used by the U.S. to carry out its foreign policy.
3.   T   F   The Peace Corps is a good example of America's moral idealism in practice.
4.   T   F   Political realism has always been the only guiding principle in U.S. foreign policy decisions.
5.   T   F   The post-war Soviet Bloc included China, Vietnam, and North Korea.
6.   T   F   The State Department's preeminence in foreign policy has gradually increased since WWII.
7.   T   F   The attentive public is less interested in foreign policy than domestic policy.
8.   T   F   U.S. foreign policy during its formative years could be described as interventionist.
9.   T   F   The Star Wars policy of President Clinton brought an end to the Communist threat.
10.   T   F   The Truman Doctrine is a clear expression of the U.S. policy of containment.

Multiple-Choice. Circle the correct response.

1.   Diplomacy differs from foreign policy in that
      a.   diplomacy is a set of techniques and strategies to achieve a foreign policy goal.
      b.   diplomacy is the all encompassing goal while foreign policy is just one aspect.
      c.   the president develops diplomacy and the State Department develops foreign policy.
      d.   diplomacy always comes first, followed by a specific foreign policy.

2.   Foreign policy based on moral imperatives is often unsuccessful for the U.S. because it
      a.   makes policymaking difficult to understand.
      b.   assumes that other nations agree with American views of morality and politics.
      c.   requires the president to establish moral standards of conduct for U.S. personnel.
      d.   makes too many enemies.

3. The foreign policy that allows the U.S. to sell weapons to dictators who support American business interests around the world, and to repel terrorism with force is the policy of
    a. détente.
    b. moral idealism.
    c. counterintelligence.
    d. political realism.

4. Edwin S. Corwin observed that the Constitution creates an "invitation to struggle" by the president and Congress for control over
    a. economic policy.
    b. appointments to the Supreme Court.
    c. foreign aid.
    d. the foreign policy process.

5. Since the Second World War almost 95 percent of the understandings reached between the United States and other nations have come in the form of
    a. protocols.
    b. legislative mandates.
    c. executive agreements.
    d. treaties.

6. The making of foreign policy is often viewed as a presidential prerogative because
    a. as opposed to making domestic policy, most presidents enjoy making foreign policy.
    b. of the president's constitutional power in this area and the resources of the executive branch.
    c. the Constitution clearly denies Congress a role in formulating foreign policy.
    d. the War Powers Act delegated this authority to the president.

7. The effect of the War Powers Act was to
    a. limit the President's use of troops in military action without congressional approval.
    b. allow the President more freedom in the use of military troops throughout the world.
    c. give the President new powers in the area of foreign policy.
    d. prevent aggressor nations from becoming too strong militarily.

8. Generally, the efforts of the President and the elites to influence foreign policy are most successful with that segment of the population called the
    a. zealots.
    b. mass public.
    c. attentive public.
    d. thoughtful public.

9. The Monroe Doctrine states that the U.S.

    a. had territorial dominion over South America.

    b. was neutral in its relations with Europe and Asia.

    c. could trade openly with China.

    d. would not meddle in European internal affairs and would not accept foreign intervention in the Western Hemisphere.

10. The strategic defense initiative (SDI or Star Wars) was a proposed program to deter nuclear war by

    a. shifting the emphasis of defense strategy from offensive to defensive weapons systems.

    b. shifting our defense to an offensive weapons system.

    c. developing more intercontinental ballistic missiles.

    d. allowing for joint U.S./Soviet Union development of manned space stations with laser guided missiles for world domination.

11. The event that signified the Soviet Union had relinquished its political and military control over the nations of Eastern Europe was the

    a. renewed interest in Cuba.

    b. fall of the Berlin Wall.

    c. defeat in Afghanistan.

    d. dissolution of the Soviet Union.

12. The end of the Cold War means that U.S. foreign policy will need to be

    a. much more stable and predictable than it has been before.

    b. directed at policing the world because the U.S. is the only superpower today.

    c. basically directed at economic aid to underdeveloped countries.

    d. much more flexible in order to deal with changing conditions and complex situations.

13. Operation Desert Storm carried out by the U.S. and a coalition of other nations lead to the

    a. overthrow of Saddam Hussein in Iraq.

    b. overthrow of the Sheikdom of Kuwait.

    c. restoration of the Sheikdom of Kuwait.

    d. overthrow of the government in Iran.

14. The Helms-Burton Act created an embargo, which remains today, against the nation of

    a. Haiti.

    b. Cuba.

    c. Iraq.

    d. Iran.

15. Concern over nuclear weapon proliferation intensified in 1998, when nuclear devices were detonated by the nations of

    a.   Israel and Palestine

    b.   North and South Korea

    c.   India and Pakistan

    d.   China and South Africa

Short Essay Questions. Briefly address the major concepts raised by the following questions.

1.   Describe the formal and informal powers of the president to make foreign policy.

2.   Trace the stages of United States foreign policy from isolationism through détente

3.   Discuss the current foreign policy challenges the U.S. faces today, besides regional conflicts.

4.   Summarize the role that the U.S. has played in recent regional conflicts.

ANSWERS TO THE PRACTICE EXAM

Fill-in-the-Blank.

1.   Foreign policy [p. 573]

2.   Diplomacy [p. 573]

3.   State Department [p. 577]

4.   Monroe Doctrine [p. 583]

5.   World War II [p. 583]

6.   containment [p. 585]

7.   military-industrial complex [p. 581]

8.   détente [p. 586]

9.   trade deficit [p. 593]

10. most-favored nation status [p. 592]

True/False.

1.   T [p. 573]   3.   T [p. 574]   5.   F [p. 585]   7.   F [p. 581]   9.   F [p. 586]

2.   T [p. 574]   4.   F [p. 575]   6.   F [p. 577]   8.   F [p. 582]   10. T [p. 585]

Multiple-Choice.

1.   a [p. 574]   4.   d [p. 575]   7.   a [p. 579]   10. a [p. 586]   13. c [p. 595]

2.   b [p. 574]   5.   c [p. 576]   8.   c [p. 581]   11. b [p. 588]   14. b [p. 594]

3.   d [p. 575]   6.   b [p. 576]   9.   d [p. 583]   12. d [p. 588]   15. c [p. 589]

Short Essay Answers

1.   Describe the formal and informal powers of the president to make foreign policy [p. 575-576].

    •   The Constitution provides the president with two main areas of foreign policy authority.

        ◊   Article II, Section 1 designates the president as Commander-in-Chief of the armed forces.

188

◊   Article II, Section 2 gives the president the power to make treaties with the consent of two-thirds of the Senate.

◊   Additional foreign policy power is granted to appoint ambassadors, other public ministers, and consuls. Section 3 gives the president the power to recognize foreign governments.

- The informal powers of the president to conduct foreign policy are his superior access to information, his ability to lobby Congress for funds, his influence over public opinion, and his head-of-state moral leadership position to commit the United States to a course of action.

2.   Trace the stages of United States foreign policy from isolationism through détente [p.581-586]

- The founders of the United States distrusted the European nations, and attempted to stay out of European conflicts and politics. This policy of isolation from Europe was well-stated in the Monroe Doctrine in 1823.

- The end of the isolationist policy started with the Spanish-American War in 1898. It continued to change in World War I when the United States intervened in a European conflict.

- Isolation returned after World War I in reaction to that conflict.

- Isolation ended forever on December 7, 1941, when the Japanese attacked Pearl Harbor, Hawaii, and the United States was thrust into World War II. The era of Internationalism had begun.

- Although the United States and the Soviet Union were wartime allies against Nazi Germany, the alliance quickly fell apart after the war. The Soviet Union wanted a divided Germany, and seized control of Eastern Europe to create a Soviet bloc, which would challenge the Western world in an ideological, political, and economic struggle known as the Cold War.

- The United States foreign policy throughout the Cold War was called "containment" of the spread of Communist nations. This was well stated in the Truman doctrine to halt Communist expansion in southeastern Europe.

- In the Cuban Missile Crisis of 1962, the United States and the Soviet Union confronted each other over the placement of Soviet missiles in Cuba. This crisis led the world to the brink of a nuclear World War III. After intense negotiations, the crisis was resolved in a peaceful manner.

- After the Cuban Missile Crisis, the United States and the Soviet Union realized that they had to reduce the threat of nuclear war. Under the leadership of President Nixon and Henry Kissinger, a period of détente or relaxation of tensions began. The first tangible result of détente was the Strategic Arms Limitation Treaty (SALT I) signed in 1972.

3.   Discuss the current foreign policy challenges the U.S. faces, besides regional conflicts [p. 588-593].

- The rapid collapse of the Soviet Union in 1991 led to profound changes in world politics. A number of new nations were created including Georgia and Ukraine. Russia remains the largest nation of the group, joined by a majority of the republics from the Soviet Union.

- Nuclear proliferation remains a world problem as more nations join the Nuclear Club. See Table 18-1 for a look at the nations with nuclear warheads.

- Terrorism has become both a domestic and foreign policy problem for the United States. Much terrorism has stemmed from the Middle East crisis between Israel and the Arab nations.

- President Nixon was responsible for opening diplomatic and economic relationships with Communist China in the 1970s. China has become a major trading partner of the United States in the 1990s. China sought and received most-favored-nation status for tariffs and trade policy from the United States. In 1997, China took control of Hong Kong from the British, and has preserved the free enterprise system.

- The global economy has created an interdependent world, in which the events of one region can effect the entire world. The political structures of the nation states, perhaps under the United Nations, must adapt and change to deal with the world of the twenty-first century.

4.   Summarize the role that the U.S. has played in recent regional conflicts [p. 593-599].

- After the collapse of the Soviet Union, regional conflicts have been a major focus for U.S. foreign policy. Some of the major regional conflict have their roots in the Cold War and have been seemingly difficult to resolve.

- The island nations of Haiti and Cuba have had a major impact on domestic as well as foreign policy issues for the U.S. Immigrants from both countries flooded into Florida. Continuing problems with the communist government in Cuba led the United States to pass the Helms-Burton Act for an embargo of Cuba.

- The Middle East crisis between Israel and its Arab neighbors has been a long-standing regional conflict. The United States has repeatedly tried to bring about a peaceful settlement of the conflict.

- The invasion of Kuwait by Iraq in 1990 has created an additional Middle East crisis for the U.S. In Operation Desert Storm, the United States with a coalition of nations under United Nations authority pushed Iraq out of Kuwait. Iraq under United Nations sanctions has continued to defy the world and created an environment of regional tension.

- The breakup of the Soviet Union lead to profound change in Eastern Europe. The former nation of Yugoslavia broke into a number of nations which were engulfed in war with Serbia, the dominant part of Yugoslavia. This war continues today, as the United States and other European nations seek a peaceful solution to the conflict.

- Ethnic conflicts have broken out in a number of African nations. The conflicts have been made more devastating because of drought and famine conditions in many countries. The United Nations and United States efforts have been unable to stop the conflicts.

Chapter 19
State and Local Government

CHAPTER SUMMARY

The U. S. Constitution and the States

The U.S. governmental system is one national government and fifty separate state governments. The U.S. Constitution reserves power to the states:

- The states may take any action not prohibited by the Constitution or given expressly and exclusively to the national government.
- States can tax, spend, and regulate intrastate commerce.
- States also have general police power to promote and safeguard the health, morals, safety, and welfare of the people [p. 607-608].

State Constitutions

State constitutions are usually long and detailed, an aspect that can be traced to the loss of popular confidence in state legislatures between the end of the Civil War and the early 1900s. In addition, framers of state constitution may have felt it necessary to fill in the gaps of the very brief U.S. Constitution [p. 608]. Changes to state constitutions are usually carried out by constitutional conventions. Eighteen states, such as California and Oregon, allow for a constitutional initiative, which provides for citizens to petition placing proposed constitution amendments directly on the ballot [p. 609].

The State Executive Branch

The tradition of powerful colonial governors in our early history has lead many state to weaken the power of state governors. The influence of Jacksonian democracy has created a large number of independently elected executive figures in addition to the governor. The election of so many officials tends to fragment executive authority [p. 609], and many states have tried to strengthen the power of their governor. A state governorship has become a stepping stone to the presidency as three of the last four presidents have served as state governors before becoming president. In 43 states state governors hold the important power of line item veto on appropriations. Congress tried to give this power to the president, but the Supreme Court of the U.S. ruled the law unconstitutional [p. 610].

The State Legislature

State legislatures have often been criticized for being unprofessional and ineffective. State legislators are often given few resources to accomplish their functions, as states limit salaries and the time the legislature can meet. In eight states, including Texas, legislators are paid less than $10,000 per year. See Table 19-1, page 612, for the characteristics of state legislatures, including salaries.

One of the major functions of state legislatures is to reapportion both state and federal legislative districts every ten years after the federal census. Gerrymandering, in which the majority party manipulates reapportionment for its own benefit, continues to be a problem.

Many state legislatures have provided for more citizen input by initiative, referendum, and recall. Under these provisions, which do not exist at the national level, citizens can directly propose constitutional, and legislative changes, and remove officials from office [p. 613-615].

The State Judiciary

Each state, including the District of Columbia, has its own court system. See Figure 19-2, page 615, for a view of a sample state court system. State judges can either be elected or appointed depending upon the level of the court and the state. State courts, which handle the bulk of cases in the United States, have severe problems of underfunding and overwork [p. 615-619].

How Local Government Operates

The U.S. Constitution makes no mention of local government. The state creates every local government. In 1811, Dillon's rule established the very narrow interpretation that local government could only possess the powers specifically given it by the state [p. 619]. The home-rule-for-cities movement against state control culminated in Cooley's rule, which advocated that cities govern themselves. Since 1900, most states allow home-rule cities to write their own city charters and govern themselves within state laws. The four major types of local governmental units are municipalities or cities, counties, towns and townships, and special districts. See Table 19-2, page 621 for the numbers and types of local governments in the U.S.

With over eighty thousand local governments in the United States, the trend toward consolidation of two or more government units into a single unit, is understandable. The most successful form of consolidation has been functional consolidation, which focuses on cooperation to provide services to inhabitants in that area.   The federal government has encouraged the use of a council of government (COG) to focus on areawide problems [p. 622]. The structure of governing cities or municipalities can be divided into four general types:

- the commission plan—developed in Galveston, Texas, and combined legislative and executive power in the hands of a small group of individuals
- the council-manager plan—centers the executive power in the hands of a professional city manager hired by the city council to run the city
- the mayor-administrator plan—used in big cities, where the mayor is chief executive but appoints an administration to do routine administrative tasks
- the mayor-council plan—the mayor is the chief executive officer. The amount of power the mayor has depends or whether it is a weak or strong mayor form of government [p. 623-624].

For much of the late nineteenth and early twentieth centuries, major cities were run by political "machines." These were usually strong mayors who used patronage to get elected and reelected. Reforms developed, including other structures of city government, such as council manager. Political machines were replaced, but they were generally much more effective in providing access to government services for economically disadvantaged city residents. Large cities have struggled to try to provide services for more and more people. Cities have tried governing the metro area as a whole, annexing suburbs, consolidating local government functions, and creating special metropolitan districts to provide specific services.

Paying for State and Local Government

State and local government provide the bulk of spending for education in this nation. See Table 19-3, page 628, for state expenditures, and Table 19-4 for local expenditures. The most important tax at the state level is the general sales tax. The major revenue source for local government is the property tax. In the 1980, many state budgets doubled as the federal government cut back on its aid to states. State governments tried two approaches to maintain balanced budgets. One was to increase taxes, and the other was to reduce spending. The states that reduced spending generally had better economies, and a number of states experienced budget surpluses [p. 629-630].

State and Local Government: Issues for the New Century

The federal government continues to give states more responsibility to solve more problems. States appear likely to give local governments more responsibility to deal with crime, pollution, and congestion. State and local governments will continue to face the challenge of providing our children with a world class education and finding the resources to pay for this education [p. 630].

KEY TERMS

charter—p. 620

consolidation—p. 622

constitutional initiative—p. 609

Cooley's Rule—p. 620

Council of government (COG)—p. 622

county—p. 620

Dillon's Rule—p. 619

general law city—p. 620

general sales tax—p. 628

home rule city—p. 620

municipal home rule —p. 620

patronage—p. 625

police power—p. 608

property tax—p. 629

referendum—p. 613

CD-ROM *AMERICA AT ODDS*

SCHOOL CHOICE IN K-12 EDUCATION. The interactive module for Chapter 19 looks at public education in the United States. Explore what kind of school you attended. Look at the history of educational views and the availability of educational opportunity. See the different views about school choice. Examine the advantages and disadvantages of school choice and make up your own mind. A ten-question interactive multiple-choice quiz reinforces key points in the material.

PRACTICE EXAM

(Answers appear at the end of this chapter.)

Fill-in-the-Blank. Supply the missing word(s) or term(s) to complete the sentence.

1. The recall and initiative are examples of _____ _____, in which the people vote

    directly on important issues.

2. State courts annually process about 100 million cases, 70 percent of which involve _____ offenses

    or other minor cases.

3. The view that cities should be able to govern themselves is called _____ _____.

4. The most successful forms of government consolidations have been _____ consolidations.

5. The _____ lets citizens bypass legislatures and propose new statutes in government.

6. A voluntary organization of counties and municipalities concerned with areawide problems is the

    _____ _____ _____.

7. The _____ form of municipal government is the oldest and most widely used.

8. Rewarding faithful party workers and followers with jobs is called _____.

9. By far the most important tax at the state level is the _____ _____ _____ and

    at the local level, the _____ _____.

10. _____ is the biggest category of expenditure at the local level of government.

True/False. Circle the appropriate letter to indicate if the statement is true or false.

1. T   F   The U.S. has more than eighty-thousand separate local governmental units.
2. T   F   Compared to the U.S. Constitution, state constitutions are surprisingly brief and rather general documents.
3. T   F   Most states follow the practice of electing numerous executive officials.
4. T   F   The states hold general police powers to protect the health, morals, and safety of their citizens.
5. T   F   Local government are considered to be creatures of the state government without independent status of their own.
6. T   F   County governments are extremely complex entities, a product of Jacksonian democracy.
7. T   F   The most numerous form of local government is the special district.
8. T   F   The major defect of the council-manager form of government is that there is no single, strong political executive leader.
9. T   F   By far the most important tax at the state level is the personal income tax.
10. T   F   Today, states have been successful in reducing their budget deficits by increasing state taxes.

Multiple-Choice. Circle the correct response.

1. The major reserved powers of the states are the powers to
    a   regulate health care, transportation, and education.
    b   control education, build highways, and provide for the general welfare.
    c   tax, spend, and regulate intrastate commerce.
    d   control the election process, charter banks, and coin money.

2.   One of the important tenets of Jacksonian democracy was

   a   the fewer public officials elected, the better the quality of decision-making.

   b   that public employees should be selected on merit, not partisanship.

   c   the more public officials elected, the more democratic the system.

   d   that the national government should be supreme in all spheres of life.

3.   According to historians, the length and mass of detail of many state constitutions reflects a(n)

   a   interest in clarifying the public good.

   b   loss of popular confidence in state legislatures between the end of the Civil War and early 1900s.

   c   high esteem for state government by the framers of state constitutions.

   d   a desire that state constitutions serve as clear guides to future decision-makers.

4.   Many governors have the power of the item veto, which they use on legislation called

   a   authorization bills.

   b   appropriation bills.

   c   general welfare bills.

   d   constitutional amendments.

5.   The initiative, referendum, and recall all represent forms of

   a   representative democracy.

   b   indirect democracy.

   c   minority rule.

   d   direct democracy.

6.   The procedure enabling voters to remove an elected official from office before his term has expired is the

   a   recall.

   b   recommit.

   c   impeachment process.

   d   referendum.

7.   Dillon's Rule states that

   a   local governments can perform any function they choose unless forbidden by state law.

   b   state government can create local government at their own choosing.

   c   local governments can exercise only those powers expressly given or fairly implied by the state.

   d   local government derives its power from the fourteenth amendment of the U.S. Constitution.

8.   The difference between a county and a municipality is that a county

   a   may not be created at the behest of its inhabitants.

   b   is always geographically larger than a municipality.

   c   can determine its own form of government.

   d   performs more important service than a municipality.

9. The union of two or more governmental units to form a single unit is referred to as a

    a   federation.

    b   unionization.

    c   consolidation.

    d   merging.

10. Local government units have addressed regional problems primarily through the organization of

    a   interstate compacts.

    b   metropolitan federation.

    c   special districts.

    d   council of government.

11. The form of municipal government that combines both executive and legislative powers in the hands of the same elected members is referred to as the

    a   mayor-council plan.

    b   commission plan.

    c   council-manager plan.

    d   mayor-administrator plan.

12. The form of municipal government that appoints an administrative officer to do routine tasks is the

    a   council-manager plan.

    b   commission plan.

    c   mayor-council plan.

    d   mayor-administrator plan.

13. Which of the following techniques helps to deal with the loss of tax base in large cities?

    a   hiring a city manager.

    b   using the commission form of city government.

    c   annexation of surrounding areas.

    d   developing a suburban growth plan.

14. The biggest category of expenditure for local governments is

    a   police protection.

    b   health.

    c   public welfare.

    d   education.

15. The major source of tax revenues at the local level is

   a   franchise taxes.

   b   general sales tax.

   c   property taxes.

   d   personal income taxes.

Short Essay Questions. Briefly address the major concepts raised by the following questions.

1. Discuss the provisions of direct democracy that many states allow in their constitution.

2. Explain the four major types of local government units.

3. Discuss the four general plans for governing municipalities.

4. Examine the basic areas of revenues and expenditures for state and local government.

ANSWERS TO THE PRACTICE EXAM

Fill-in-the-Blank.

1. pure democracy [p. 573]

2. traffic [p. 573]

3. Cooley's Rule [p. 577]

4. functional [p. 583]

5. initiative [p. 583]

6. Council of Government [p. 585]

7. mayor-council [p. 581]

8. patronage [p. 586]

9. general sales tax, property tax [p. 593]

10. Education [p. 592]

True/False.

1. T [p. 573]   3. T [p. 574]   5. F [p. 585]   7. F [p. 581]   9. F [p. 586]

2. T [p. 574]   4. F [p. 575]   6. F [p. 577]   8. F [p. 582]   10. T [p. 585]

Multiple-Choice.

1. a [p. 574]   4. d [p. 575]   7. a [p. 579]   10. a [p. 586]   13. c [p. 595]

2. b [p. 574]   5. c [p. 576]   8. c [p. 581]   11. b [p. 588]   14. b [p. 594]

3. d [p. 575]   6. b [p. 576]   9. d [p. 583]   12. d [p. 588]   15. c [p. 589]

Short Essay **Answers**

1. Discuss the provisions of direct democracy that many states allow in their constitution [p. 613-615].

   - State constitutions allow direct democracy in initiative, referendum, and recall.

   - Legislative initiative allows citizens to circulate a petition to place an issue on the ballot. A certain percentage of the registered voters in the last gubernatorial election are required to place the item on the ballot

   - A referendum is similar to the initiative, except that the issue is proposed first by the legislature and then directed to the voters for their approval. This is most often used for local bond issues and amendments to state constitutions.

   - Recall is the right of citizens to remove an elected official from office before their term has expired. Citizens must circulate petitions and get a certain number of signatures to place the recall on the ballot.

2. Explain the four major types of local government units [p. 620-622].

   - The four types of local governments are municipalities, counties, towns and townships, and special districts.

   - Municipalities are a political entity created by people to govern themselves locally. Municipalities rely on financial assistance from state and national government.

   - Counties are local governments set up as political extensions of state government. Counties apply state law and administer state business at the local level.

   - Towns in New England states are governing units that combine the roles of city and county in one unit. The word town can be used as just another name for a city. The New England town is unique to that part of the country. Townships are somewhat like counties. Unlike New England towns, they are rural governments only.

3. Discuss the four general plans for governing municipalities [p. 623-624].

   - The four general plans are (1) the commission plan, (2) the council-manager plan, (3) the mayor-administrator plan, and (4) the mayor-council plan.

   - The commission plan, which originated in Galveston, Texas, concentrates legislative and executive powers in the hands of city commissioners. Each commissioner is individually responsible for heading a particular city department. The mayor is one of the commissioners, and has only ceremonial powers.

   - In the council-manager plan, the city council appoints a professional manager, who acts as chief executive. The mayor may be a member of the city council or not, but has only ceremonial powers.

- The mayor-administrator plan is often used in large cities where there is a strong mayor. The mayor appoints an administrative officer, whose function is to free the mayor from routine administrative tasks.
- The mayor-council plan is the oldest and most widely used. It consists of a mayor, who is an elected chief executive, and the city council is the legislative body. There are two sub-varieties, the weak mayor and the strong mayor. About 50 percent of American cities use some form of the mayor-council plan.

4. Examine the basic areas of revenues and expenditures for state and local government [p. 628-630].

- Both state and local government spending are concentrated in the areas of education, public welfare, highways, health, and police protection. Education is the biggest category of spending. See Tables 19-3 and 19-4, page 628.
- The most important tax revenue at the state level is the general sales tax. The property tax is the most important revenue source at the local level. Non-tax revenues include federal grants, publicly operated businesses, court fines, and increasingly state lotteries.
- In the 1980s and 1990s, with the national government shifting more responsibility to the states, state governments were having problems balancing their budgets. Two approaches were tried, increasing taxes, and reducing spending. Generally, the states that reduced spending, had better economic growth.